The BTO Nestbox Guide
by Chris du Feu

Design and production
Derek Toomer

Published by the British Trust for Ornithology

British Trust for Ornithology
The Nunnery
Thetford
Norfolk
IP24 2PU
01842-750050
www.bto.org

First published in 2003
© 2003, British Trust for Ornithology, Thetford

ISBN 1-902576-81-0

Text: Chris du Feu
Design & layout: Derek Toomer
Printed by Crowes, 50 Hurricane Way, Norwich NR6 6JB

Front cover: Great Tit by Howard Lacey. Title page: Robin by Graham Roberts

Contents

*T*hanks to the dedication of the BTO, the awareness and appreciation of Britain's wild bird life is growing at a time when many species, like the House Sparrow, are under serious threat from man-made as well as natural factors.

Intensive agriculture, increasing urbanisation, climate change and pollution... all are causes of problems for birds. One such problem, in particular, is a steady reduction in the availability of safe nesting and roosting sites. The removal of live and decaying trees, the renovation of rural buildings and modern house building techniques all contribute to this loss. To increase awareness of this growing problem, the first National Nest Box Week was launched in 1997 with the slogan "Britain Needs More Holes". Today this need is greater than ever.

Everyone has a role to play in helping preserve Britain's wild birds. An ideal starting point is to offer the warmth, security and shelter of a soundly constructed nestbox where birds can raise their young. You don't need a large garden - Blue Tits, for example, are present in virtually all gardens and will take readily to nestboxes. In this immensely helpful book you'll find all the information you need to help you construct, position and maintain your box, plus a wealth of additional facts about the birds that could soon be nesting inside. You'll be rewarded with an increase in the numbers and diversity of birds visiting your garden, and you'll be playing an important part in the conservation of our natural heritage, too.

At Jacobi Jayne & Company we are delighted to support the BTO's efforts in encouraging the provision of more nesting and roosting sites. Enjoy this guide...and enjoy the exciting variety of wild birds in your garden.

Graham Evans

JACOBI JAYNE & COMPANY

Acknowledgements

The writing and publication of this guide has depended on the contributions of many people, BTO members and others, over many years. It has drawn heavily on previous editions of the BTO guide *Nestboxes*, the first edition of which was published in 1952. I am deeply indebted to the generous way in which so many have given of their hard-won experience. The BTO is fortunate indeed to have such a pool of knowledge from which to draw.

In addition to the contributions which have been acknowledged in the earlier guides, the following have helped with details of the designs in this new publication G Fisher, Geoff Lynn, Colin Shawyer and Ken Woodgate. At all stages of production, the following BTO staff have been closely involved and given their invaluable help and expertise: Graham Appleton, Peter Beaven, Nick Carter, Dave Leech, David Glue, who also wrote the introduction. Tim Bernhard has produced the artwork for the exploded diagrams and associated illustrations. Photographs include some from the BTO collection and others which have been taken specifically for this guide. The photographers were Derek Belsey, Ian Carter, Chris du Feu, Darren Frost, John Harding, George Higginbotham, Tommy Holden, Tony Jenkins, Howard Lacey, Chris Mead, Rick & Vanessa Newman, Dorothy Norman, Jill Pakenham, Colin Paton, Graham Roberts, Colin Shawyer, Moss Taylor, Mike Toms, Derek Toomer, David Waistell, Nicholas Watts, Mike Weston, Ken Woodgate. A detailed list of their contributions can be found in the appendices.

Derek Toomer has been responsible for the design and the desktop publishing for the book and his skill has turned my initial ideas into a reality far more attractive than I had envisaged possible. His work has included much effort in finding suitable illustrations and his adeptness with image manipulation software has considerably enhanced both the aesthetic appeal of the illustrations and their instructional value.

I am most grateful to all those contributors listed above, without whom this book would still only exist in the imagination. Thank-you.

How to use this book

The organisation of this Guide is very different from previous editions of the BTO guide *Nestboxes*. It is hoped that readers will find the layout and cross-referencing easier to use. Species accounts have been grouped by box design and the readiness with which they will utilise boxes. The key (inside front cover) lists species in alphabetic order for quick reference and also gives a summary of box design for these species.

A comprehensive guide to all British nestbox-using species would be an unwieldy publication and this guide concentrates instead on species which are most likely to be found in gardens and woodland. It is intended that guidance notes for other species (which are listed in the Appendix) will be published on the BTO website in the near future.

Although some of the photographs included do show the standard nestbox design, many do not. This is deliberate. Birds are adaptable and will use a wide range of box designs variations. By examining the differences in nestbox design you will see that boxes can be adapted to suit the wood available rather than sticking slavishly to exact plans which require pieces of expensive, new wood of precisely the right dimensions.

Several species accounts include graphs indicating population trends constructed using data gathered by a number of long-term BTO surveys. All graphs, therefore, indicate changes in relative abundance over time rather than absolute values of population sizes.

Species Boxes — explanatory notes

The coloured box at the top of each species page provides details of the most appropriate box design and summarises the status, distribution and breeding ecology of each species.

Nestbox – The most suitable nestbox design including, where relevant, details of hole diameter.

Distribution/Status – 'Distribution' refers to the habitats and regions in Britain where the species may be found. 'Status' refers to the conservation status of the species based on recent trends in abundance and the international importance of the population, as indicated in the *Population Status of Birds in the UK* report. This is published every five years by the UK's leading bird research organisations. Red-, amber- and green-listed species are of high, moderate and low conservation concern respectively. The background colour of the species box indicates the species' conservation status.

Siting – Appropriate height and location for the nestbox.

Nest – Description of a typical nest, although construction may vary according to materials available.

Eggs – Typical numbers of eggs in a clutch and brief description of egg colouration. Note that a few clutches may fall outside the range, particularly if they are abandoned before completion.

Density – Typical territory size. This can be used as a rough guide to the density at which boxes should be placed, but territory size may vary greatly, depending on factors such as habitat quality and abundance.

Incubation – Length of the incubation period and the sex or sexes responsible for incubating. Later clutches may be incubated for shorter periods than those produced earlier in the season.

Nestling – Length of period from hatching to fledging. Again this may vary according to weather, food supply, brood size and amount of disturbance.

Broods – Typical number of broods produced per season. Figures in brackets indicate that the species may occasionally be multi-brooded.

Phenochart – explanatory notes

The 'phenochart' at the foot of each species page indicates the timing and length of the typical **laying** (blue bar), **incubation** (yellow bar) and **nestling** (black bar) periods for the UK population. The faded ends of each bar represent the period during which only a few pairs may be performing a particular activity. The solid bars indicate the peak period during which a relatively large proportion of the population will be engaged in that activity.

Nests and nestboxes

Introduction

Introduction

The aim of this *Nestbox Guide* is to provide details about the construction, siting and maintenance of a variety of types of nestbox suitable for those common garden birds that regularly use boxes, cavities, ledges and other artefacts provided by Man in gardens, whilst providing useful information that will help you to chart the nesting fortunes of the box occupants. This Guide provides step-by-step illustrated instructions for constructing the most suitable boxes for each of these species. The Guide also outlines box designs for several less common garden nestbox users, such as Tawny Owls and Redstarts, and gives some information about boxes for birds in surrounding environments, particularly in woodland and farmland.

A Great Tit assesses a potential nesting site.

Robins use a variety of artificial sites. This one is nesting in a discarded kettle.

This Guide does not claim to be the final word on nestboxes. Like its predecessors, it has drawn on the experience of many BTO members and others, spanning some 70 years. The BTO welcomes further suggestions, designs and knowledge accrued from practical experience, in order to enhance any future edition.

Please send any ideas or additional information to the Nest Records Officer at BTO, Thetford, Norfolk IP24 2PU (*nest.records@bto.org*). Very many thanks — and do enjoy your nestbox making and watching.

Why put up nestboxes?

Nestboxes have a long and interesting association with Man and homestead. It is still possible to find Norman-French *colombiers* — thick-walled open topped towers with scores of nesting holes for Feral Pigeons built into these walls from floor to top. The nesting and roosting pigeons, with their long breeding season, provided meat throughout the year. How times have changed!

Houses and gardens have many potential sites for nesting birds as well as providing opportunities for artificial nest sites. What nesting birds do you think this property supported? (See p11 for answers)

Arguably, the case for providing nestboxes in and around our gardens has never been greater. Changing weather patterns and damage caused by floods and storms (as in 1987, 1990 and 2002) associated with global climate change, the use of pesticides and herbicides, the increasingly sanitised and hostile agricultural landscape, habitat destruction due to urban development and over-zealous home improvements are just some examples of the huge number of potential threats currently faced by the UK's birds.

Much of our agricultural landscape is of little value to nesting birds.

Although the provision of boxes alone will not solve the problems of pollution or climate change, where a lack of nesting sites is the factor that is limiting breeding populations, nestboxes can provide an instant, but long-term, solution. A nestbox, accepted and successfully used by a pair of Blue Tits, House Sparrows or Starlings within your own garden, can therefore provide one of the simplest ways to help the UK's threatened birdlife. The sight of young birds fledging from a nestbox never fails to lift the human spirit, whether for a casually interested home-owner or an avid birdwatcher.

The potential for nestbox provision is great. The 20 million homes within the UK currently occupy an area greater than that of all our nature reserves combined, providing an increasingly diverse and important habitat that is literally on your doorstep. The BTO's various garden bird surveys have shown that gardens in both towns and villages will, on average, attract some 20 species of bird to supplementary food at winter bird tables. Typically, however, fewer than half of these species, stay to nest. Sadly, few gardens contain trees with holes large enough to house Great Tit or Starling nests and many birds leave in spring to nest in adjacent woodland cover. Shrubs and hedges can be planted in gardens and will rapidly provide suitable nest sites for open-nesting Blackbirds and Greenfinches, but it takes several decades of mature tree growth to create a cavity big enough for Tawny Owls or Stock Doves to breed in. Most gardens are just too small to provide trees of sufficient size and age to form such natural nest sites.

What makes a good nestbox?

A wide range of species requires cavities in which to nest. Each species has its own particular requirements, although birds can be remarkably versatile and opportunistic,

Features of good nestbox design

- Boxes should be durable.
- Boxes should exclude avian and mammalian predators.
- The contents of the nest should be shielded from extremes of weather.
- Box design should facilitate the inspection of nest contents without disturbing the breeding attempt.
- Boxes should be simple and cheap to construct while bearing in mind the welfare of the occupants.

Birds are adaptable and use a wide range of artificial sites, including many provided unintentionally.

seeking out the most unexpected nest sites if insufficient natural holes are available. Starlings have been known to use security alarm systems, Spotted Flycatchers have built nests in peg-baskets, Wrens have occupied hanging flower baskets and Great Tits have nested in post boxes. This Guide does not attempt to list all the artefacts which have been used by nesting birds, but rather aims to provide a sound, practical portrayal of tried and tested nestbox designs.

Although the cutting diagrams provided indicate precise measurements, birds are generally not so selective and nestbox constructors should be willing to stray from the exact dimensions given, according to the wood available. Designs may also be modified to accommodate local requirements — prevailing weather, extremes of climate, particularly active local predators, competing species and availability of materials. Some species may also show different nestbox preferences in different places. For example, in some areas, Tawny Owls nest readily in standard large hole entrance boxes whereas in others they may favour a 'chimney' box.

Nestboxes are not always used immediately after they are erected. Although your resident pair of inquisitive, territory-holding Robins, may inspect a newly installed nestbox within an hour and take to it quickly, another box may remain empty for several years and may need to be repositioned. This has dented the aspirations of many, but patience is essential for the nestbox maker. The learning process of particular birds may be slow but the potential rewards for the observer are very great.

If your local Blue Tits do not nest in your nestbox straight away, it is still unlikely to remain completely unused. Birds such as tits, Starlings and sparrows often shelter in boxes at night, safe from the extremes of weather and predators such as cats, foxes and Tawny Owls.

Boxes are especially important during prolonged periods of bitterly cold winter weather. Small birds can huddle together at night, reducing the impact of rain and wind-chill. At dusk, Wrens may gather from far and wide, 60 or more cramming into a single nestbox. Your box may make the difference between the short-term extinction and survival of a local population. In addition, the nestbox that supports no wildlife whatsoever is most unusual indeed. Bats, dormice, wood mice, voles, moths, bees, spiders, slugs and many other animals use them as welcome, safe hiding or nesting places. In return, they enhance the colour, sights, sounds and biodiversity of your garden.

Recording information about nesting birds

Regularly monitored nestboxes can yield a wealth of information crucial to our understanding of the basic biology and population ecology of birds in a rapidly changing environment. In recent years, large-scale nestbox projects in woodland and farmland habitats have helped to unravel the population dynamics of species such as tits, Kestrel and Tawny Owl. Individual home-owners have also played an important role by charting the fortunes of birds using their garden nestboxes and submitting this information to the BTO's Nest Record Scheme (NRS).

The NRS gathers information collected by volunteer nest recorders about the productivity of individual breeding attempts of both box- and open-nesting species, forming a vital part of the BTO/ JNCC Integrated Population Monitoring Programme which assesses the changing fortunes of the UK's avifauna. For further details about the NRS, and to find out how you can participate, see chapter *Making your watching count* or contact the Nest Records Officer at BTO Thetford HQ (*nest.records@bto.org*).

Nestboxes can help to encourage community spirit and enhance wildlife interest. As they are fairly easy to produce, it is possible to call on non-ornithological talent. Manpower can be drawn from various sources — schools, adult education classes, wildlife reserve volunteers and prisons. Sponsorship can provide a good way to raise funds. An annual summary of the events taking place in nestboxes, in a newsletter or parish magazine, rarely fails to generate awareness and interest. Home-made nestboxes also make ideal, practical gifts for people of all ages.

Finally, the therapeutic benefit of nestboxes should not be underestimated.

Gardens, parks, hospitals and green spaces dotted with actively used nestboxes help to educate, enhance a caring attitude and aid physical and mental healing among stressed humans. Just as birds benefit, so will humans — from the inquisitive youngster, through the energetic conservation worker, to the house-bound elderly or disabled.

Starling nestlings, under a week old, still blind and featherless in their untidy nest of dried grass and feathers (— only their mother could love them!).

House and garden nest sites

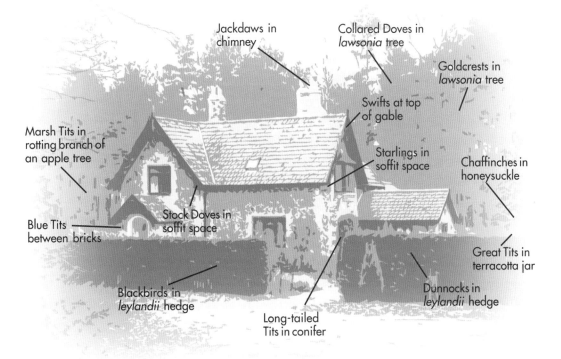

Jackdaws in chimney

Collared Doves in *lawsonia* tree

Goldcrests in *lawsonia* tree

Swifts at top of gable

Marsh Tits in rotting branch of an apple tree

Starlings in soffit space

Chaffinches in honeysuckle

Blue Tits between bricks

Stock Doves in soffit space

Great Tits in terracotta jar

Blackbirds in *leylandii* hedge

Dunnocks in *leylandii* hedge

Long-tailed Tits in conifer

(All the above nested in this house and garden in three seasons)

Nestbox construction and maintenance

Where to site nestboxes

Construction of nestboxes

Care, maintenance and safety

Where to site nestboxes

The highest priority when siting any nestbox must be to provide a safe, comfortable environment in which birds can nest successfully. This aim often suffers from conflicting demands: box location must facilitate access for nesting birds, whilst simultaneously providing shelter from extremes of the elements and deterring any would-be predators. All boxes should also be positioned such that maintenance and cleaning is as simple as possible, and if records are to be kept, ease of inspection must also be considered in order to minimise the risk of disturbance to nesting birds. For boxes in gardens, it can be a bonus if they are placed where they can be observed easily, as great pleasure and interest may be derived even from casual observation of the nesting process. In addition to these general considerations, certain species may have specific preferences, making an ideal situation for one undesirable for another. Such individual requirements are dealt with in the main species pages.

Fixing boxes to artificial structures

Attaching boxes to man-made structures in gardens is simpler than fixing them to trees, as the growth of the tree does not have to be taken into consideration (see below). Screws or nails can be used:

- Masonry nails can be used to attach boxes to walls. Galvanised nails are preferable to wire nails for attaching boxes to wooden structures because they last longer.
- Screws are preferable to nails as they are less likely to become loose. Stainless

Nails: A – copper, B – galvanised steel, C – aluminium, D – wire, E – annular ring.

steel or brass screws will last longer than steel screws and all screws will last longer, and be easier to remove eventually, if they are smeared with oil before use.

Alternatively, if you are planning an extension to your house or performing other building work, boxes can be built directly into walls or roofs (see *Construction of nestboxes* section). Whereas nests of Starlings or House Sparrows under the roof tiles may bring detritus and pests into the house, boxes built into the walls provide a secure environment for these declining species to nest in without fouling the inside of your home.

Boxes for Swifts built in loft space of house with entrances through the gable end. The back of the boxes are removed to show multiple nesting chambers.

It is generally not advisable to mount small boxes on poles. Although this can provide a site well protected from mammalian predators, the nest will be very obvious to avian predators. It may also be exposed to extremes of elements, enduring the direct heat of the sun and the worst of the wind and rain.

Fixing boxes to trees

While vegetation may provide a greater degree of shelter and concealment from potential predators than man-made structures can offer, no method of fixing boxes to living trees is entirely foolproof and boxes attached to trees will require regular attention.

Nails and screws —
- Fixing a horizontal or vertical batten to the back of the box using screws or nails helps keep it away from the tree,

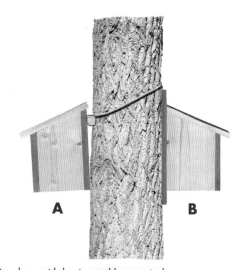

A   **B**

A – box with horizontal batten tied to tree.
B – conventional box with overlong back pegged to tree.

preventing water running down the trunk and into the box (above left).

- Nails and pegs can be used to attach the box to the tree, but these will gradually be pushed out of the trunk as the tree grows and boxes must therefore be inspected annually. Holes that fit the nails snugly should be drilled in the batten to prevent it splitting when the nails are hammered through it. The use of flat-headed nails, not tapered or oval-headed nails, is recommended as these will be pushed out with the batten as the tree grows rather than being pulled through it.
- Alternatively, screws may be used. These will not be pushed out but may need to be slackened as the tree grows and therefore again require annual attention. However, screws may be very difficult to adjust in softer woods such as sycamore.
- Steel nails and screws are susceptible to rusting and therefore should not be used. Nylon, aluminium or hardwood nails are preferable alternatives, as they will not damage chainsaws if accidentally left in the tree after the box is removed.

All nails and screws **must be removed** when the box is taken down. If you are putting up boxes on other peoples' property, remember to consult them about methods of attachment.

Do not use nails or screws in commercial timber as they will damage the

trees, damage saws and possibly injure the workers using the saws.

Tying boxes —

- Wire may be used to tie boxes to the trunks of trees, but it will need to be checked annually to ensure it does not constrict tree growth or become embedded in the tree.
- Robust rubber bands (cut from large inner tubes) do expand, allowing the tree to grow, but are susceptible to perishing and may be gnawed through by squirrels or mice.
- Synthetic twine is both elastic and long-lasting (although some baler twine is now biodegradable and may not last more than a year or two) and is also relatively cheap and simple to use. Boxes may be loosely tied, the twine making an angle of 30☐ or so upwards around the trunk (see diagram above left). To allow for growth merely edge the box upwards a little each year. Again, squirrels and mice may be able to chew through the twine.

If neither nailing/screwing nor tying are viable options for nestbox attachment it is possible, in some situations, to wedge boxes firmly into tree forks or bushes.

Box location

Nestboxes are obviously most urgently needed in places where natural holes are scarce but where food is plentiful. Such places include managed woodland where mature trees are cropped and dead wood removed, farmland with the tall trees removed from hedgerows and with old buildings cleared, young forestry plantations and many gardens.

Aspect — The direction that the box entrance faces makes relatively little difference provided that it is sheltered from prevailing wind, rain and strong sunlight. Your patio sun-trap may not be suitable for nesting birds! In the most exposed gardens, the sector from north through east to southeast is possibly the most favourable. In shady woodland other considerations, such as the slope of the trunk, are likely to override that of direction. In cold, north-facing woodlands, boxes may be best facing southeast in order to catch the early morning warmth from the sun. It is important to keep boxes away from the wet side of a tree trunk, often identifiable as the side that has the greatest coverage of green algae (but if in doubt wait for rain). To give additional shelter to the entrance of small boxes, angle them downwards slightly, particularly if the nestbox roof has only a short overhang.

A bad design of box sited badly — the wide wall allows a cat to sit and reach into the over-large, low entrance hole.

A – correctly sited box, sloping forwards slightly giving shelter from elements.
B – incorrectly sited box, more exposed to elements.

Height — For many species the height of the box is not critically important and may range from 1 m upwards, depending on ease of inspection, visibility, etc. Boxes high on tree trunks are less easy for marauding humans to reach, but may be more visible than lower boxes concealed in the shrub layer of a wood. For most species the nestbox must be sited to allow a clear flight path. Notes on the different species give more detailed guidance where appropriate.

Reducing access for predators — If possible, boxes should be located away from predators, although this may be impossible in many cases — weasels, for example, can climb almost anything. Boxes in gardens must be placed where cats cannot climb, which can make wall-mounted boxes safer than boxes in trees. Prickly or thorny bushes also make good sites for some species, although inspection can be awkward.

Box density

The optimum density of boxes will depend on the habitat and species involved. A good plan is to begin by erecting about ten assorted small boxes per hectare, making sure that they are more or less uniformly spaced, and then keep adding boxes each breeding season until some remain unused.

Colonial species, such as Starlings, may nest very densely, and so boxes should be erected in clusters. A column of identical nestboxes mounted on a telegraph pole could, however, be a recipe for confusion of potential occupants, so where possible, nestboxes should be placed at different heights, on different trees and facing in different directions.

Boxes designed for non-colonial species should not be erected at such a density that they encourage aggressive behaviour between close neighbours. If you find most of your boxes are occupied successfully, you should consider erecting some more.

Feeding stations

Studies have shown that provision of supplementary food at all times of the year does enhance the breeding performance and the survival rates of young. However, garden nestboxes should never be placed near to bird tables or other feeding devices. Large numbers of feeding birds will disturb potential nesting pairs and attract predators. **Ornamental boxes with integral bird feeding tables, often sold in garden centres, must be avoided.**

Re-siting

Occasionally boxes are not used for several years after siting. It may be worth re-siting unused smaller boxes after three or four years and larger boxes after six or more years.

'Bed and breakfast' — a bad design. Always keep feeding and nesting places separate. Can you spot the other faults with this box? (See p18 for answers.)

When to put up nestboxes

Traditionally, nestboxes for small birds are put up in the early spring. Indeed, *National Nest Box Week* always starts on 14th February, St Valentine's Day, when the birds are reputed to start courtship. Many people find it is helpful to have a fixed time of year when nestboxes are put up or checked for the forthcoming season, and there is no better time than the second half of February.

However, some species may start prospecting for sites long before this date. Juvenile birds may even begin to select potential nesting sites throughout their first autumn and winter when they are exploring their surroundings. In addition, boxes may be used by roosting individuals at any time of year. Even boxes put up in summer are therefore unlikely to remain completely unused. In many cases it is best to put up boxes as soon as they are available. How many unused nestboxes lie in garden sheds in the 'I was going to . . .' heap? Put it up now!

Deterring predators

The contents of a nestbox may represent an easy meal to a variety of avian predators (Great-Spotted Woodpeckers, Carrion Crows, Jays, Magpies, Tawny Owls, Little Owls) and mammalian predators (cats, grey squirrels, wood mice, weasels) and steps may need to be taken to ensure that eggs and nestlings are adequately protected from predation by these species.

Box location — In gardens, the chief mammalian predators are likely to be cats and grey squirrels. The best defence against these is to site boxes where they cannot be reached. A plain wall is as safe a place as any, although squirrels may still climb the brickwork or drain pipes. Remember that some mammals can jump considerable distances, so ensure that any boxes cannot be reached by a single jump from the ground or a nearby branch.

Suspending boxes by wire may also help to deter less agile mammalian predators such as cats. Placing a metal cone around the wire will prevent grey squirrels, mice and weasels from sliding down it in the manner of a fireman sliding down the pole.

Preventing purchase — A box on which the predator is unable cling may be the next line of defence. A covering of plastic, formica or metal may help, although grey squirrels can gnaw through formica and plastic once they gain a foothold. Such coverings will also add to the weatherproofing of boxes. Prickly twigs and steeply sloping roofs may deter some predators, particularly cats, from sitting on top of the box and lying in wait for adult or fledgling birds as they fly out of the entrance hole.

Reinforcing entrance holes and box walls — Grey squirrels and Great Spotted Woodpeckers often gain access to boxes by enlarging the entrance hole. If the wood available for making the nestbox is of varying thickness, using thicker, harder wood for the component with the entrance hole may help to reduce this problem. Entrance holes may also be reinforced or repaired by placing metal plates around them.

Some predators, particularly Great Spotted Woodpeckers, can break through the sides of wooden boxes in order to eat the eggs or nestlings inside. Woodpeckers usually gain access low down in the box at the level of the nest cup to take the young. Damage is worst in years when natural invertebrate food is in short supply as young woodpeckers are hungrier and nestlings tits and flycatchers noisier and easier to find. Unfortunately, once a woodpecker has discovered nestboxes as a food source it may continue to attack them in later years. Some workers have prevented woodpeckers attacking boxes by covering them in rubber sheeting which is too springy for the birds to hammer through.

The safest commercially available box is made from a cement and sawdust

Box with entrance hole reinforced with a metal plate to prevent enlargement and entry by grey squirrels.

compound (Woodcrete) and hangs from a branch or bracket by a wire. Woodcrete is too hard for any predators to break into.

Woodcrete box manufactured by Schwegler, hanging from wire to hamper access by predators.

Deterring reaching predators — Large mammalian predators and Great Spotted Woodpeckers may predate nestlings by reaching in through the entrance hole with their forelimbs or bills respectively. Deep boxes with high entrance holes will maximise the distance between predator and nest

contents, although sometimes tits will fill a deep box nearly to the top with nesting material. Predators reaching into the box whilst sitting on the roof will find it much harder to reach round into the box if the roof overhang is extended and the hole is placed as high as possible on the front of the box. A ledge placed just inside of the entrance hole allows nestlings to hide where marauding mammals cannot reach. Deep boxes also prevent woodpeckers taking young at the entrance as they jump up hoping for food.

A ledge below the entrance hole prevents cats' paws reaching to the nest and may allow eggs or young to remain hidden from weasels.

Small mammals such as mice and weasels can be prevented from entering boxes by fixing a wide angled funnel (which could be made from a plastic food container) or a short length of tubing at the entrance hole. Some workers have suggested this reduces the desirability of boxes to birds: it certainly makes them more conspicuous to humans.

Open-fronted boxes — Crows, Jays and Magpies, and sometimes Little and Tawny Owls, will take the contents of open-fronted boxes. The best protection against these predators is a balloon of 40 mm chicken wire or a grill of stiff wire of about 200 mm radius around the front of the box (see next page). However, weasels, being very slender, will still be able to penetrate these defences.

Deterring mammals — Some mammals, including weasels and squirrels, are deterred by smell but birds seem not to be. Anti-cat and dog pellets, obtainable from garden centres, can be used to deter pets from approaching boxes. Cat scarers, which emit

Chicken wire supported by a spring steel framework protecting an open fronted box from predation by birds.

high frequency sound when cats, dogs etc. are detected, may also keep some mammalian predators away. Local gardening folklore may be a source of useful ideas — why not try them?

Predation by humans — Remember that humans can also be serious 'predators', particularly as their attentions are often systematic, whether the aim is casual vandalism or serious egg stealing. Unfortunately, measures which make boxes more predator proof can make them more

visible to humans. The best defence against nest destruction by humans is to make sure that boxes are well-concealed high in trees hidden by leaves, or low on the trunk hidden by the woodland scrub layer, rather than placed at the traditional 3 m on a bare tree trunk. In some extensive schemes, nestboxes have been numbered at random to confuse humans wishing to interfere.

Jay, the 'Gentleman Poacher', often steals eggs and young from unprotected nests.

Spot the errors

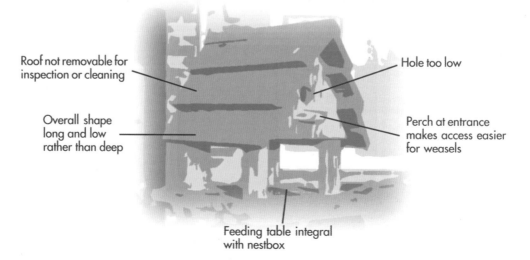

Roof not removable for inspection or cleaning

Overall shape long and low rather than deep

Hole too low

Perch at entrance makes access easier for weasels

Feeding table integral with nestbox

Construction of nestboxes

Tools

The only specialist tool needed will be one for boring circular entrance holes.

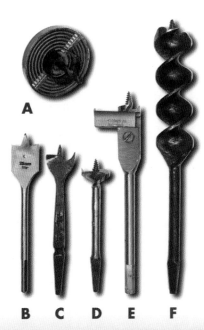

Making holes: A – hole-saw, B – high-speed flat bit, C – centre bit, D – screw-nose centre bit, E – expanding bit, F – twist bit.

A set of hole-saws is the most economical and versatile attachment for a power drill, allowing a variety of hole sizes to be made. However, drill bits for use in hand braces, hand drills and power tools are also available. Obviously, a single bit is only able to produce one size of hole. If you are only making a few boxes and do not want to

Hand-held brace and bit boring entrance hole.

Electric drill with hole-saw cutting entrance for tit box.

go to the expense of buying a range of bits, choose a 32 mm bit as this will potentially allow any of the common small birds, including the declining House Sparrow, to use the box. An expanding bit is more expensive but can be used to cut various sizes of holes.

Materials

Wood —

- Wood is the best material to use when constructing nestboxes.
- Any wood used should be at least 15 mm thick in order to provide sufficient insulation and to prevent warping.
- Boxes built from more resilient hardwood may be less susceptible to the elements but softwood is much easier to work.

Suitable pieces of wood can often be obtained for free, or at least very cheaply, from timber merchants' scrap heaps. It may be even cheaper to use second hand timber, such as old floorboards, pallets and packing cases. With any second hand timber, beware of nails when handling and cutting the wood. People living on the coast may be able to use driftwood, including fish boxes or packing cases that may be almost ready-made to use as nestboxes.

If buying new wood for nestboxes, ensure that it comes from a renewable source. There is no point in improving the habitat for our birds at the expense of even more endangered habitats elsewhere.

Manufactured boards — Most manufactured boards, including chipboard, hardboard and blockboard, are only suitable for boxes located under shelter, such as boxes built within the roof space of a building. However, marine and exterior grade plywoods are much more resistant and can be used in any location. Both these materials are very long lasting but are expensive if purchased new.

Metal — Metal is a very good conductor of heat and therefore a very poor insulator. Metal boxes also suffer from severe condensation, dampening the nest and its contents. Metal is therefore not a suitable material with which to construct nestboxes.

Plastic — A variety of ready-made small plastic designs are available. Many are ingenious or attractive but are of limited value to birds due to their poor insulation qualities, overheating rapidly in the sun and quickly becoming cold at night. In addition, predation may be a problem as grey squirrels and other rodents may be able to gnaw through even thick plastic sheets and small boxes made completely from plastic will also suffer condensation.

Plastic boxes with some wood components may be satisfactory. Several workers use wooden boxes with recycled plastic board for roofs only. This has the advantages of being waterproof, durable and keeping rain off the wooden parts of the box. Other people report that such boxes have a lower take-up rate than wooden boxes and that the nests still become wet with condensation. However, larger tough plastic drums with sufficient drainage holes and placed in shaded sites have been used successfully by larger birds such as Stock Doves, Jackdaws and Tawny Owls.

Construction methods

Grain — Where possible, the grain of the wood should run vertically down the side of the box to help rainwater drain more rapidly. Drainage can also be improved by mounting the floor of the box just above the lowest point of the side panels so that water drips off the sides rather than seeping into the end grain of the wooden base (see photograph below). Try to avoid leaving the end grain exposed horizontally, as rainwater will easily seep into it, encouraging rot and decreasing the life expectancy of the box.

Floor of nestbox should be inset slightly, aiding drainage and prolonging life of wood.

Waterproofing and drainage —
Waterlogging of the nest represents a serious risk to eggs and nestlings, potentially leading to chilling and possibly in extreme cases, to chicks drowning. It is therefore essential to ensure that boxes are as waterproof as possible. If two narrow pieces of wood are to be joined along their length they should be tongued and grooved or rebated to stop wind and rain entering the box. Water entering the box should also be able to drain freely, so if the floor of the box meets the walls in watertight joints it is a good idea to drill small drainage holes in the floor.

Assembling boxes — Wood may be fixed together with nails or screws, although nails are both easier to use and cheaper. In wetter parts of the country and in damp situations iron nails may rust long before the wood of the box has rotted. Galvanized nails or brass screws should therefore be used. In wet areas it may also be useful to seal top and side joints with waterproof glue, but never rely on glue alone for any joints, and never seal the floor joints, as this will prevent proper drainage. If you are constructing boxes from

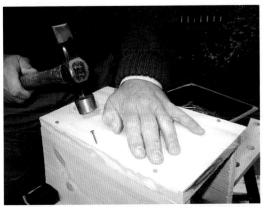

Nails driven in at an angle hold better than those driven straight in.

materials. These also provide a barrier to the elements and are easier to fit than ready-made hinges, but some materials are prone to perishing after a few years.

Metal hinges are more durable, but those with steel parts are liable to rust and may require repeated oiling. Brass hinges are expensive.

Brass hinges attached to the outside of the box allow the roof to overhang on all four sides.

plywood, try to avoid screwing or nailing parallel to the laminations as the layers may split apart.

Opening lids or fronts — Boxes should have a means of easy access for both inspection and cleaning. Apart from the interest provided by observing the progress of a nest, boxes can provide valuable information for national recording schemes. Access may be gained through a hinged or removable roof or through an opening front — which system you use is a matter of personal preference. Opening fronts allow a more waterproof roof, but can be less wind proof lower down the box. Boxes with opening fronts must also be inspected more carefully to prevent nest contents from falling out and to stop the young from fledging prematurely.

Hinges — Cheap hinges can be made from old tyre inner tubes or other flexible, synthetic

Boxes with removable roofs are easier to inspect than those with hinged ones, and this may be an important factor where many boxes are to be inspected regularly. Removable roofs, like those with outside hinges, also allow an overhang on all four sides, which helps to protect the box from the sun and rain.

Roofs — Removable or hinged roofs may be fixed or fastened securely using hooks and eyes, loose fitting nails used as locating pins (see next page) or by gravity (use a heavy stone) according to taste and circumstances.

A conventional top-opening box with hinge of rubber cut from an old inner tube. The lid is secured by soft wire wound round a nail.

Box with removable lid secured by loose-fitting nails passing through sides of box into the batten under the roof.

Alternatively, simple catches can be created from three staples — two on the box, one on the lid — and a locking nail or by using soft wire wrapped round a nail (see below).

A simple roof-locking device made from three staples and a nail.

For extra rainproofing, roofs can be covered with roofing felt, vinolay or rubber from old inner tubes.

Perches — In general, perches are a hazardous feature on small and medium sized boxes and should not be fitted. They are not needed by birds (with some exceptions given with the notes for appropriate species) and they can provide a potentially disastrous foothold for predators.

Varying the designs — While the cutting diagrams provided in this guide are based on standard wooden planks, it is easier, cheaper and more effective to make boxes according to wood available rather than to adhere slavishly to the exact plans shown. Dimensions of nestboxes, other than the entrance hole diameter, are generally not critical and may be varied according to the sizes of wood available. As a general rule, for small birds, the box needs to be big enough for your fist to reach inside in order to clean the used nest at the end of the season.

Rustic boxes and designer boxes — Boxes made from hollowed logs are difficult to

Box made using bark-covered off-cut. This maintains natural appearance and is thickest at the entrance, where squirrels are most likely to attack.

construct, difficult to inspect and often lack sufficient weatherproofing. There is no evidence that they are preferred to any other type of box (except by humans).

Many garden centre boxes (thatched roof with integral feeding table, etc.) are of fundamentally bad design, incorporating perches, over-large holes set too low down in the front of the box, fixed roofs which are neither watertight nor allow boxes to be cleaned out at the end of the season and often offer incredibly small nesting cavities. There are no real benefits in using these boxes, which are often very expensive indeed.

Rustic design — bad for the birds and probably expensive.

Built-in boxes

Nestboxes incorporated into the structure of buildings can be long-lasting and fairly maintenance free. They are a permanent fixture, leaving homes for the birds after the original human owners have moved on and provide controlled nesting spaces which may be preferable to the untidy, pest-ridden and inaccessible nests that can be built under the eaves of house roofs.

Although some new building developments incorporate places for birds to nest, this should not be thought of as a new idea. The earliest built-in nestboxes were designed for pigeons and built into farm buildings in order to give a supply of meat throughout the year. Happily, modern designs are made with environmental rather than utilitarian motives, using ready-made commercially available nestboxes that can be incorporated into structures as they are being built. We can now see Kestrel boxes on mobile phone masts, roofing tiles with nesting holes for Swifts and building blocks with nest holes that take the place of bricks in a wall. Details of such designs can be obtained from wildlife product suppliers and

some manufacturers of roof tiles and building blocks.

Built-in boxes can also be produced by leaving an appropriately sized hole in a wall during construction, leading to a box attached to the inside face of the wall. If the entrance hole required is smaller than the gap left by the missing brick, insert a piece of wood with an appropriately sized hole cut out of it. Boxes placed within roof spaces do not need to be of the same heavy, weatherproof construction as do those produced for exterior use, nor do they need a sloping roof to repel rain, and may therefore be adapted from readily available, discarded packing cases. A thin plywood tea chest, for example, will be quite suitable for Jackdaws, the only modification required being the construction of an inspection hatch.

A Swift box made from thin plywood, projecting through hole in brickwork of the gable end of the loft space.

Birds which nest on ledges or in open holes can simply use the hole left when a brick is removed from a wall, a thin strip of wood placed across the lower part of the front of the hole preventing the nest and its contents from falling, or being blown out. Such sites would be suitable for Spotted Flycatchers, Pied Wagtails, Wrens or Robins, depending on the exact location of the hole and the amount of vegetation cover.

Care, maintenance and safety

Preserving boxes

Wood preservatives — Any wood preservative helps prolong the life of a box. Many non-toxic, water-based preservatives are now available. Traditional oil-based preservatives are not recommended because of their potentially toxic properties. Whatever preservative is used, ensure the boxes have dried before they are put in place so that birds' feathers are not fouled by wet residue. Do not treat the insides of boxes because the long-term effects of preservatives, if any, on birds are not known. Boxes can be camouflaged to some extent by treating with preservatives of two colours.

Repairs to boxes — Check all boxes in the late winter to make any necessary repairs before the breeding season. Minor repairs can often be made on the spot. A kit consisting of hammer, pincers, nails, string and formica or metal patches is adequate for many jobs, including dealing with holes enlarged by squirrels. Major repairs are best carried out by putting up replacement boxes and taking the damaged ones for repair in a workshop. In places where grey squirrel or woodpecker damage is frequent, it will pay to reinforce the entrance with a metal plate before the box is put up.

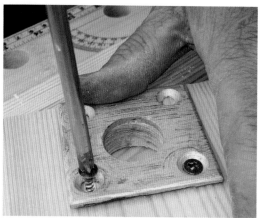

A metal plate protects the entrance from attack by squirrels or woodpeckers.

Parasites

Fleas — Bird nests, however attractively they may appear to be built, are often infested with parasites. The major parasites in the majority of nestbox nests are fleas (*Siphonaptera*), which are widespread and can occur in great numbers. There are several species, but all are adapted to living with birds rather than with mammals and, therefore, their bite is usually irritating to humans rather than harmful. After birds have fledged, flea pupae remain in the nest and will hatch during the following year.

An abundance of fleas emerging from a used nest and waiting on the nestbox to jump onto a passing bird.

Flat-flies — Swift, Swallow and martin nests can contain high infestations of flat-flies (*Hippoboscidae*). These flightless insects over-winter in nests as larvae, then emerge as adults when the birds return in spring. Nests in natural or man-made sites, which are used year after year, can contain flat-fly populations large enough to affect the health of the nestlings.

Prevention — Nothing can be done to reduce parasite numbers during the breeding season. However, when the breeding season is over, all boxes should be cleaned and the contents thrown some distance away. The action of ejecting the material forces premature hatching of fleas and scattering contents at some distance helps to prevent them from returning to the box. This also reduces their chance of survival.

The bird protection law (DoE Licence WLF1000068) states that birds nests must not be cleaned and nests should not be collected before 1st August. For tits, cleaning of the nestbox contents is best carried out as soon as possible after the young have fledged (but not before 1st August). Some other hole-nesting species, including sparrows, may have second and third broods in the same nest. The nests of these species should be left until some time during the autumn when it is certain that they are no longer in use. It is a good idea to clear their nests well before the winter because the birds may need to use the box as a winter roosting site and may even build a new nest for roosting.

A small, stiff-bristled brush (such as an old tooth brush) or a scraper will be useful in cleaning the corners of boxes where debris may have accumulated and hardened.

Nestbox co-habitants

Bird nests support a wide range of species, mostly invertebrates, the majority of which have little effect on the birds but are there only because the box provides a suitable niche for them. Such creatures include earwigs (*Dermaptera*), tree slugs (*Lehmannia marginata*) and various moths (*Lepidoptera*). Sometimes these species occur in such great numbers that they must irritate the nesting birds, but for the most part they are of little consequence to them.

The tree slug often uses nestboxes for sheltering and resting places. This benign species often shares boxes with nesting birds.

Rove beetles (*Staphylinidae*) and spiders (*Araneae*) prey on other invertebrates and, therefore, may benefit the birds by removing some of their parasites. In addition, scavenging animals, including woodlice (*Isopoda*) and sexton beetles (*Silphidae*), effectively help to clean the nest cavity.

Competing nestbox users

Some animals use nestboxes to the exclusion of birds. They may occupy the boxes before birds select them, or may evict birds which have already started to nest.

Invertebrates — Wasps (*Vespidae*) occupy empty boxes, filling them with their spectacular papery nests. There seems little point in destroying a wasp nest unless it is a direct hazard to humans as the wasps will only nest elsewhere, possibly preventing other birds from nesting. The presence of a wasp nest in your garden may have some benefits — wasps spend much of their time preying on small, insect garden pests.

The beginnings of a wasp nest suspended below the roof of a small nestbox.

Some solitary bumble bees (*Bombidae*) may evict the avian inhabitants of a box and occupy the lining of nests, creating domed chambers. As many bee populations are now under serious pressure, nests in boxes should be left alone and not cleared. A number of manufacturers now produce nesting boxes for a variety of insects including bees. Erecting these may reduce the chances of cavity nesting birds being ousted from their nest sites.

Hornet

Mammals — Mice, voles, shrews and bats sometimes use bird nestboxes. The fact that mammals use bird nestboxes indicates a lack of natural sites for them too. If there is competition for your boxes, one solution is to put up purpose-built mammal boxes. Designs are widely available for bats and dormice (for example, from the Mammal Society).

Provision of nesting materials

Birds can spend enormous amounts of energy foraging for nesting materials. Many gardens, though well provided with nestboxes, may be so manicured that nest building materials are hard to find. Extra energy spent by birds in searching elsewhere for materials may result, eventually, in fewer young surviving. Help can be given by ensuring that there is material available.

Patches of moss in the lawn will remain green throughout the year and provide one of the most important materials for many box-nesting birds. Nest lining material can be provided artificially and bundles of suitable material can be purchased from various pet food and wildlife product suppliers. Feathers are also useful for lining nests but may now be less readily available to birds because fewer people keep hens at the bottom of the garden. Rather than putting that old feather pillow in the dustbin after your spring cleaning, let the birds have the stuffing. Birds are remarkably adaptable about what they can use for nesting material. My mother recalls that within a week of the first dropping of aluminium foil 'window' from RAF bombers as they flew over occupied Jersey, Blackbirds were using the material in their nests. Be careful, however, not to provide material containing long threads, as these may become entangled in the legs of nestlings, cutting off the blood supply to the growing legs. Worse still, the chicks could become shackled to the nest and left to starve to death after their siblings have fledged. Long, non-biodegradable synthetic fibres or long, coarse animal hairs (such as pony tail) are the worst offenders.

Several species including Swallows, martins and various thrushes use mud as a building material. In spells of dry weather during spring and summer, you can ensure a constant supply of mud by filling an upturned dustbin lid with a mixture of earth, water, lime and, if available, cow dung and dried grass. House Martins take mud from the edges of pools or streams, so make your pool look like the real thing with soft mud around the edges and water in the centre. Alternatively, in large gardens a natural pond with gently sloping edges will provide the mud required.

Human safety

The long term interests of birds will not be well served by unsafe activities of nestboxers — after all, an injured nestbox enthusiast cannot do much for the birds. Many activities concerned with nestboxes are potentially hazardous — even the apparently simple act of nailing a tit box to a house wall. The notes below highlight a few specific points to bear in mind when making, erecting or checking nestboxes:

- Be familiar with the safe working practice for any tool that you use.

- Do not use implements, particularly power tools, for purposes for which they are not intended.

- Do not use power-saws on reclaimed wood where there is any possibility of striking a nail.

- Wear protective clothing when using masonry nails or inspecting Tawny Owl boxes.

- Beware of electricity, whether it is in an overhead wire under which you are carrying an aluminium ladder or an unprotected power cable in the garden shed to which you are nailing a nestbox.

- Ensure ladders are secure before you climb them. Be particularly careful of ladders against thin trees or ladders resting on branches projecting from the main trunk of a tree.

It is impossible to list all precautions that should be taken and this is by no means a comprehensive list. Common sense is a far better guide than a book full of detailed policies and rules.

Care must also be taken when cleaning out nestboxes. Although many birds' nests represent amazing feats of natural engineering and are aesthetically pleasing, this outward attractiveness can hide very real health hazards. Nestboxes can act as breeding grounds for a variety of organisms, mostly fungi growing on the damp nest material, that may cause human respiratory diseases. When cleaning out boxes, be careful not to inhale dust from the nest contents, avoid bringing used nest materials indoors and always wash your hands after handling used nests.

Monitoring and conservation
Making your watching count

Making your watching count

Britain has a long tradition of naturalists, often amateur, including such pioneers as Gilbert White, who have studied the lives of birds for many years. You might therefore think there is little about Britain's avifauna that we do not already know. Nothing could be further from the truth. There is still every reason to study the behaviour and ecology of even our most common birds.

Monitoring and conservation of bird populations

The amount of time and money that can be invested in protecting the environment is finite. Conservation efforts must therefore be effectively and efficiently directed towards those species that are under greatest threat. In order to achieve this goal, population monitoring to identity those species that are in decline, those that are stable and those that are increasing in number is essential. Population monitoring therefore enables changes in the relative abundance of species over time, known as population trends, to be calculated.

In any monitoring scheme, it is important to record information from all parts of the country and from all habitats to avoid biasing the results. Population trends may be different in different regions and habitats. Recent work has shown, for instance, that Blue Tits breed earlier but rear fewer young in gardens than in woodland. A survey that includes no gardens will therefore not give a representative picture of the breeding success of the species across the whole country.

Monitoring schemes should cover species that are currently abundant as well as those that are uncommon or rare, as the future welfare of common species cannot be assured and data cannot be collected retrospectively. The House Sparrow, for example, was regarded as a pest only 20 years ago but has since declined in numbers to the point where it is uncommon or absent in many gardens.

Monitoring the abundance of species is useful when identifying those that are in need of help, but in order to help conserve these species it is important to identify the causes of any observed population declines. Changes in bird populations may be driven by survival rates, migration patterns and/or productivity. By recording events in nests, you will be collecting vital data about avian productivity that may help to determine the reasons for the decreasing abundance of a particular species.

Nest Record Cards for red-listed species are particularly valuable. This card shows the history of a Marsh Tit nest where all seven young fledged successfully. The simple coding system, used to record nest contents and activity, is explained in the *Nest Record Scheme Handbook*.

How can your observations help?

Casual observations of birds made by one person are, on their own, of interest but of limited value, as small data sets and geographical biases may lead to results that are not representative of the country as a whole, but merely of the local population.

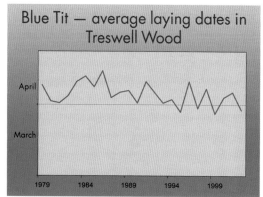

Blue Tit — average laying dates in Treswell Wood

Long-term studies at one site showing breeding becoming earlier in recent years. Is this the result of climate change?

However, if these observations are combined with those of many other people in a systematic way, the whole data set becomes far more valuable than just the sum of its individual contributions.

The British Trust for Ornithology (BTO) was founded in 1933 with the aim of collecting and analysing these types of data. The organisation now holds records spanning more than 70 years and possesses a lifetime of experience in dealing with records from many observers, both amateur and professional.

Work over the last 20 years has benefited enormously from the use of computers. Analyses, which would not have been possible before, are now taking place as a matter of routine. Increasingly, archival data sets are being computerised so that they can contribute further to the long-term analysis of UK bird populations. Of particular relevance to the nestbox user is an on-going survey:

The Nest Record Scheme

The Nest Record Scheme (NRS) was founded in 1939. Records are collected from the whole of the United Kingdom and Ireland with, typically, 30,000 nests being recorded each year by volunteer nest recorders. Participants are asked to record a set of standardised details for any nests they find, including information about habitat, nest contents and the timing of reproduction. Whether participants record a single Blue Tit nest in the garden or hundreds of nests in a larger study area, all nest records are of value and will be used. Because the scheme aims to record the breeding performance of our birds, it is important that all active nests are recorded even if they end in failure.

Participation in the scheme is free. Information is recorded in a standard format and full instructions are given in the *Nest Record Scheme Handbook* which is sent to all recorders on registering. Traditionally, records of nests have been submitted to the BTO on printed cards, with one card completed for each nest. However, records can now also be submitted electronically using the Integrated Population Monitoring

Reporter (IPMR) package. IPMR provides a more efficient method of entering data and also helps nest recorders to produce reports and analyse their own data more easily. Importantly, the package also allows recorders' data to be transferred to the central NRS database more quickly and cost-effectively, allowing their records to be put to good use more rapidly.

Recording events in nests is fascinating (but be warned, it can become addictive). Even after recording many nests over many years, birds may still surprise us. For instance, after 25 years of recording events in nestboxes, I witnessed for the first time a Wren nest which was built in a box still in use by a roosting hornet and, in another box, a successful Tawny Owl nest was followed by three successful broods of Stock Doves in one season.

A surprising event — two Blue Tit nests in a single box.

If you are interested in participating in the Nest Record Scheme or would like further information, please contact the Nest Records Officer (*nest.records@bto.org*) at BTO, The Nunnery, Thetford, Norfolk, IP24 2PU.

Guidelines for recording nest record information

All nesting birds, their eggs and their nestlings are protected by law. Bird nests should be watched and enjoyed from a distance unless records are being kept for a specific purpose such as the Nest Record Scheme.

Rare breeding birds are given special protection under Schedule 1 of the Wildlife and Countryside Act (1981). It is an offence to disturb, or even approach, a Schedule 1 bird at the nest. Licences, in order to nest record such species, can be obtained by contacting the Licensing Officer in the BTO Ringing Unit.

When visiting a nest site, the welfare of the birds is paramount. Most bird species are fairly tolerant of disturbance, although extreme caution should always be exercised, particularly during the earlier stages of the nesting cycle.

Recent scientific studies have shown that, provided care is taken when collecting data, regular visits made by nest recorders do not reduce the likelihood of a nesting attempt being successful.

Nest recorders are expected to follow the code of practice outlined in the *Nest Record Scheme Handbook*, so please make sure that you follow them closely.

As most birds have little or no sense of smell, the presence of human scent around the nest will not cause direct disturbance.

However, mammalian predators do have a keen sense of smell and can follow tracks made by people, so take care not to lead them to a ready food source.

Multiple visits to a nest vastly enhance the value of records as they allow calculation of daily nest failure rates. Visits to record progress may be made as often as once a day with very tolerant birds, but this level of recording is not required for general NRS data collection. Ideally, visits should be timed to coincide with the key events in the nesting cycle as shown in the box below.

When inspecting boxes closely, care should be taken to avoid inhaling any dust or other matter from old nests. Boxes may contain keratin-eating fungi that can also grow in the warm, damp human lung and are not easy to remove. It is also easy to catch various intestinal disorders from nest

Recording key events in the nesting cycle

1 Building. This is best observed from a distance.
2 Afternoon visits to find date of first egg. Small birds usually lay one egg a day until the clutch is complete and their eggs are normally laid in the morning. A new egg found in the afternoon will be most likely to be the egg of that day.
3 One visit during incubation to establish the total number of eggs laid. Another visit, nearer hatching, will allow the observer to record the number of eggs that are still present and whether they are being incubated.
4 Two or three days after hatching to record the number of eggs hatched.
5 Two-thirds of the way through the nestling period to record the number of nestlings that hatched successfully.
6 Fledging date. Best observed from a distance as too close an inspection at this time may force a premature departure.
7 After fledging. Record the number of unhatched eggs and dead young remaining (although some dead young may have been removed by parent birds).
8 Check about weekly for signs of a second clutch (multi-brooded species only).

contents. Always wash your hands after dealing with nests.

BTO garden bird surveys

As well has gathering information on changes in the breeding success of birds, we also need to find out how the size of bird populations is changing. The BTO does this by monitoring bird populations in a wide range of habitats, including gardens. Gardens are an important habitat for many bird species, partly because their total area occupies a significant proportion of the country and partly because some other habitats seem to be deteriorating in their suitability for some bird species.

The BTO currently collects information on garden bird populations through two surveys. The first of these, the Garden Bird Feeding Survey, gathers information from a sample of 300 hundred gardens spread across Britain and monitors the use made of bird tables and hanging feeders during the winter months. This has been running since 1970 and has charted the long-term decline of once familiar species like House Sparrow, Starling and Song Thrush.

The other BTO project looking at garden birds is Garden BirdWatch, which currently involves some 16,000 people, all keeping a simple weekly record of the bird species using their gardens throughout the year. Such observations enable BTO scientists to investigate how birds use different types of gardens, and how this use varies between seasons and years.

Further information on these two projects is available by writing to the BTO, by telephoning 01842-750050, by e-mailing *gbw@bto.org* or by visiting the BTO website (*www.bto.org*).

Birds as environmental indicators

Birds are one of the most appropriate animal groups to use as indicators of the state of the environment. They are highly visible, are found across a wide range of habitats, require no specialist equipment to watch and respond rapidly to environmental changes. In the past, miners used Canaries to give early warnings of dangerous gases in the mine. Using the observations, from many recorders, of many species, we can now use our wild bird populations to give us similar early warnings of developing environmental problems.

Recent studies investigating the ecological impact of climate change in the UK provide a very good example of the use of birds as environmental indicators.

The rate at which global temperatures are rising at present is remarkable. Data collected by the Nest Record Scheme, run through the JNCC/BTO partnership agreement, have shown that the nesting season of a wide range of bird species has advanced significantly over the past 25 years. For some species, such as the Great Tit, this advance is as much as half a day per year. These observations are supported by data indicating a similar advancement in the flowering dates of plants and the emergence dates of butterflies. On the strength of these results the laying dates of both Chaffinch and Robin, which are closely correlated with spring temperatures, are now used by the Government as two of a suite of climate change indicators.

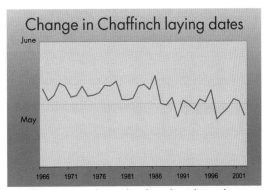

Chaffinches, together with Robins, have been showing earlier laying dates. This is now officially used as an indicator of climate change.

Nestbox designs and species

- Small hole-entrance nestboxes
- Medium hole-entrance nestboxes
- Large hole-entrance nestboxes
- Special hole-entrance nestboxes
- Small open-fronted nestboxes
- Large open-fronted nestboxes
- Papier-mâché nestboxes

Small hole-entrance nestboxes

Blue Tit
Great Tit
Marsh Tit
Coal Tit
House Sparrow
Tree Sparrow
Pied Flycatcher
Nuthatch
Redstart

Exploded view

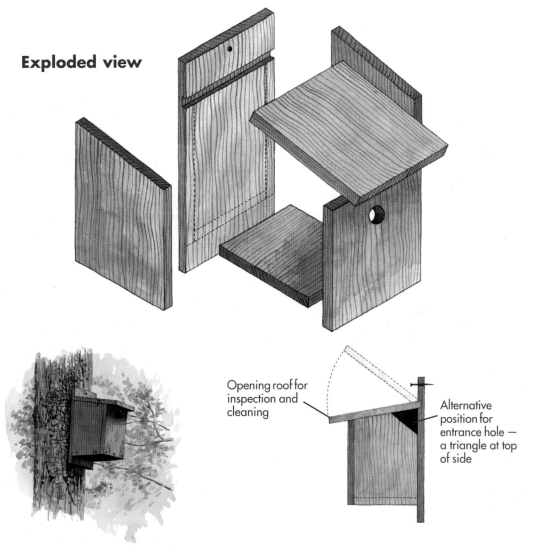

Opening roof for inspection and cleaning

Alternative position for entrance hole — a triangle at top of side

Small hole-entrance nestboxes

Roof

The box must have a watertight roof and side joints but the base construction should allow for drainage. The roof should project over the entrance to provide shelter and shade — a roof which projects over all sides will provide additional protection from rain. Sloping roofs are not essential — boxes are often fixed so that the entrance hole is angled downwards slightly, providing additional shelter and allowing rain to drain off. Inspection is normally achieved through the roof of smaller boxes.

Entrance hole size

For most small birds the only critical factor in construction is the diameter of the entrance hole. This will determine which species are able to enter. Small holes exclude larger species, rather than attracting the smaller ones — birds can use oversize but not undersize holes. An entrance diameter of 32 mm will allow access to all our common small, hole-nesting birds. A diameter of 25 mm will give access only to the smaller tits and, possibly, to Tree Sparrows.

Entrance hole position

The exact position of the entrance hole is unimportant as long as it is at least 120 mm above the floor of the box. A hole which is too low will allow predators, such as cats, to reach in to take the nestlings. Deep boxes also help prevent premature departure by restless or frightened young. The entrance hole may be positioned either at the front, or at the side, of the box. Ensure, however, that when the box is in position the hole is sheltered from the elements and is far enough away from obstructions to allow the birds an easy flight path. Some workers prefer to cut a triangular entrance hole in the rear top corner of the box, rather than to bore a round hole.

Overall size

As a rough guide, boxes should be large enough in cross section to allow access to an adult human hand. This will allow cleaning of the box and, if a trained and licensed person is available, ringing of the young. Larger boxes may provide extra space for larger broods but excessively large boxes force the birds to find a great deal of nesting material.

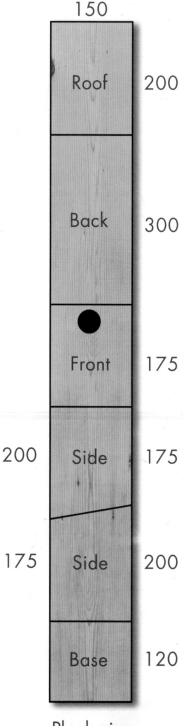

Plank size
150 mm x 1170 mm
(All dimensions in millimetres)

Blue Tit — *Parus caeruleus*

Nestbox	Small hole-entrance box, 25 mm diameter hole
Distribution/status	Present almost everywhere with shrubs or trees. Green
Siting	1 m – 5 m with clear flight path to nest entrance
Nest	Moss lined with any soft, locally available material
Eggs	7–16; all white with a variable amount of speckling
Density	Smallest territory 0·5 hectares
Incubation	13–14 days, by female
Nestling	18–19 days
Broods	1

Blue Tits are our most familiar and frequent users of nestboxes in gardens.

Boxes may be sited almost anywhere in suitable habitats. In gardens, ensure that boxes are not sited in sun traps such as exposed south facing walls, nor in sites exposed to extreme conditions such as in wind-tunnels between houses. If cats are a problem in gardens, ensure the boxes are mounted high enough to be out of their reach and that there are no opportunities for them to reach the box by climbing along roofs, wall-tops or branches.

Blue Tits generally approach their nest site from a distance and fly straight into the nest hole so ensure that they have a clear flight path to the entrance. Do not put a perch on the box as it could help weasels, or other predators, to gain access.

When siting boxes in gardens, think about the gardening activities you engage in during the nesting season. Do not site a box close to the busiest part of the garden but do site it where you can see and enjoy it from a distance.

Where possible, the box should be placed near to trees or shrubs. These can support the caterpillar crops on which the nestlings will be fed.

Blue Tits can lay large clutches, although this collection of 19 eggs was probably laid by two females.

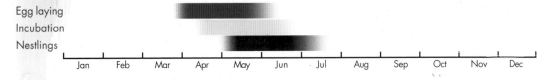

	Jan	Feb	Mar	Apr	May	Jun	Jul	Aug	Sep	Oct	Nov	Dec
Egg laying												
Incubation												
Nestlings												

Great Tit — *Parus major*

Nestbox	Small hole-entrance box, 28 mm diameter hole
Distribution/ status	Present throughout the UK and Ireland where trees provide food and nesting sites. Green
Siting	1 m – 5 m with clear flight path to nest entrance
Nest	Small twigs or coarse dried roots base, covered by moss and lined with any soft, locally available material
Eggs	5–12; all white with a variable amount of speckling, often more at one end than at the other
Density	Smallest territory 0·5 hectares
Incubation	12–16 days, by female
Nestling	18–24 days
Broods	1–2

Great Tits are larger than our other tit species and can dominate at the bird table or nestbox. However, by erecting a variety of boxes with 25 mm, 28 mm and 32 mm holes, you will provide nesting sites for the smaller tits which are not accessible to the Great Tit, you will provide sites for the Great Tits which are not accessible to House Sparrows, and you will still provide some sites for the House Sparrows.

Great Tits will nest successfully in a standard tit box cut according to the cutting diagram, but larger boxes will give them more room and they may rear slightly larger broods. The design can be modified by making the sides wider, giving a larger floor area. Boxes over about 6 litres in volume will give no additional benefits. (To calculate the volume, multiply internal width by internal depth by internal height measured at half way from front to back. If all these measurements are in centimetres, divide by 1,000 to convert to litres.)

Great Tits often use smaller cavities for winter roosting. If you build larger nesting boxes, ensure there are some standard-sized boxes with 28 mm holes in which they may roost in winter.

If Tree Sparrows oust your Great Tits, try building much deeper boxes (up to 50 cm) for the tits. Sparrows tend to avoid these (but ensure you also have additional boxes for the Tree Sparrows, whose populations were declining until recently).

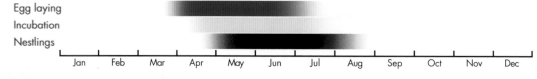

	Jan	Feb	Mar	Apr	May	Jun	Jul	Aug	Sep	Oct	Nov	Dec
Egg laying												
Incubation												
Nestlings												

Marsh Tit — *Parus palustris*

Nestbox	Small hole-entrance box, 25 mm diameter hole
Distribution/ status	England and Wales but absent from much of northwest and the area between the Humber and the Mersey. Red
Siting	Low, provided cats are not a danger
Nest	Moss lined with any soft, locally available material
Eggs	6–8; all white with a variable amount of speckling
Density	Smallest territory 2 hectares
Incubation	13–14 days, by female
Nestling	16–18 days
Broods	1

CBC/BBS population index

Even within their main range, Marsh Tits are rarely found in coniferous woodland or urban areas. They are a red-listed species because their population has declined by over 50% in the last 25 years. Marsh Tits are very sedentary and this means that it may be some years before they colonise apparently suitable areas with sufficient nesting holes if there are no nearby populations.

Marsh Tits are small and may suffer in competition from Blue and Great Tits. In order to ensure they have boxes available

A brood of 10-day-old Marsh Tits, still only partly feathered, trying to be inconspicuous by burrowing into the nest lining.

there are three steps which may be taken: provide an excess of boxes suitable for other tits; make some boxes with 25 mm entrance holes; site some boxes very low, almost at ground level.

An alternative design, attractive to both Marsh and Coal Tits that can be made from a log of wood is described on page 39.

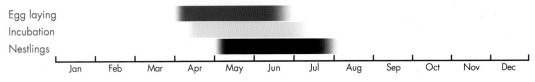

Egg laying
Incubation
Nestlings

Jan Feb Mar Apr May Jun Jul Aug Sep Oct Nov Dec

Coal Tit — *Parus ater*

Nestbox	Small hole-entrance box, 25 mm diameter hole
Distribution/ status	Absent only from treeless areas. Green
Siting	Low, will nest higher if there is no competition for nest sites
Nest	Moss lined with any soft, locally available material
Eggs	7–11; all white with a variable amount of speckling
Density	Smallest territory 2 hectares
Incubation	13–14 days, by female
Nestling	16–17 days
Broods	1 (2)

Coal Tits will nest in standard tit boxes provided for Blue Tits, but tend to prefer boxes sited nearer the ground. If predation from cats is not a concern, boxes may be placed right down to ground level. Boxes sited on isolated conifer trees in predominantly broad-leaved woodland are sometimes selected.

If competition from Great or Blue Tits is a problem, ensure that there is an excess of boxes with 25 mm entrance holes.

An alternative design, which is also attractive to Marsh Tits, can be made from a log of wood. Hazel logs of at least 10 cm diameter have proved long-lasting and effective. The photographs on the next page show the construction of the 'box' which simulates a broken-off stump of a sapling and can remain unnoticed even by the most determined vandal. It may even be worth stuffing the inside with soft, rotten birch in the hope of attracting Willow Tits.

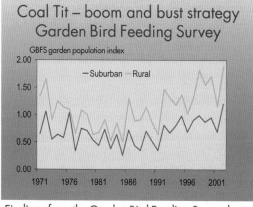

Coal Tit – boom and bust strategy Garden Bird Feeding Survey

GBFS garden population index

Findings from the Garden Bird Feeding Survey have shown how Coal Tits in gardens vary in numbers from year to year. This depends, in part, on the naturally available food, beech mast in particular.

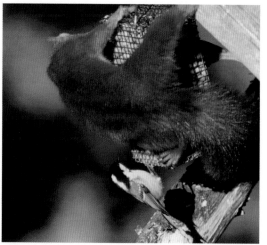

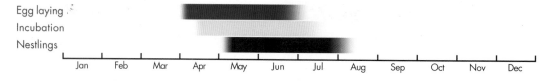

Egg laying	
Incubation	
Nestlings	

Jan Feb Mar Apr May Jun Jul Aug Sep Oct Nov Dec

Small hole-entrance nestbox made from log

1 Saw the top from the log. The sawn off section will form the roof.

2 With a chisel, split a front panel away and bore a 25 mm entrance hole in it. This panel should be about 150 mm high.

3 Hollow a cavity in the top of the log behind the panel. Leave 5–10 mm thickness of wood for the walls of the cavity.

4 Replace the front panel with loosely fitting locating nails, so that the front is removable for inspection and cleaning. Alternatively, nail the front panel in place permanently and carry out inspection and cleaning by opening the lid.

5 Replace the top using a nail as a pivot. For the removable front version, another two loosely-fitting nails are required to lock the front in place.

6 Site the finished stump in the ground.

Design by G Fisher

Exploded view of the stump-box, showing the cavity, front panel and pivoting roof.

The stump-box with roof pivoted for inspection or cleaning.

The completed box, here standing unobtrusively in coppiced woodland.

House Sparrow — *Passer domesticus*

Nestbox	Small hole-entrance box, 32 mm diameter hole
Distribution/ status	Absent only from remote parts of Scottish Highlands. Red
Siting	Avoid disturbed sites. Place boxes on trees or buildings at 2 m or above
Nest	An untidy domed structure of almost any material available, but occasionally a cup only. Lined with feathers, hair and wool
Eggs	3–6; whitish or pale blue with darker spots
Density	Can nest in colonies but box entrances should be at least 15 cm apart
Incubation	9–18 days, mainly by the female
Nestling	11–19 days
Broods	1–4

CBC/BBS population index (England)

In former years, House Sparrows were often regarded as a nuisance. However, over the last 25 years the population has declined steeply and the species is now red-listed. House Sparrows are now uncommon in many places where they were abundant in the recent past.

In spite of their close association with mankind, House Sparrows are sensitive to disturbance at the nest. Boxes should be placed at least 2 m above ground level preferably where they will not suffer constant disturbance from human activity.

Although House Sparrows will nest in open-fronted boxes, hole-entrance boxes are preferable, offering greater seclusion, security against predators and shelter from the elements.

House Sparrows build untidy nests of dried grass which may be bulky and will take full advantage of larger boxes. They usually raise more than one brood in a year and will reuse the nest site for later broods. Used nests should not, therefore, be cleaned until the very end of the season.

House Sparrows may nest colonially. Some home-owners have had success with House Sparrow terraces and these are now available from some suppliers of wildlife products.

Double-decked House Sparrow terrace with provision for 24 nests. Inspection is through opening fronts.

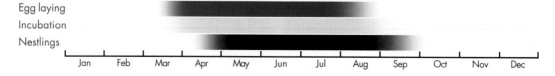

	Jan	Feb	Mar	Apr	May	Jun	Jul	Aug	Sep	Oct	Nov	Dec
Egg laying												
Incubation												
Nestlings												

Tree Sparrow — *Passer montanus*

Nestbox	Small hole-entrance box, 28 mm diameter hole
Distribution/ status	Absent from much of Scotland, western England, Wales and most of Ireland. Red
Siting	Avoid disturbed sites. Place boxes on trees at 2 m or above
Nest	An untidy domed structure of dry grasses lined with feathers
Eggs	4–6; whitish with brown blotches or speckles. Eggs tend to be smaller, browner and more rounded than those of House Sparrow
Density	Nests in loose colonies, boxes may be sited on adjacent trees
Incubation	12–14 days, by both sexes
Nestling	12–15 days
Broods	2 (3)

CBC/BBS population index (England)

Tree Sparrows are a red-listed species whose population has declined by over 50% in the last 25 years, although the recent trend indicates a recovery.

They are very sensitive to disturbance but, where they are present, they are relatively easy to attract to nestboxes. Because of the species' colonial behaviour, nestboxes can be placed close together. Tree Sparrows typically take to nestboxes fairly quickly but after three or four years the nestbox colony may dwindle or vanish. Some workers have suggested siting a second batch of boxes in a loosely spaced group some distance away from the original colony if it begins to decrease.

Tree Sparrows begin to select sites for nesting during the previous autumn and they use boxes for roosting during winter. They may even build nests for roosting and these nests may be used for rearing young the following spring. Thus, boxes for Tree Sparrows are best put in place in the autumn.

You will know when a former roost site is about to be used for nesting because the sparrows usually place freshly picked, small green leaves in the nest before laying eggs.

Tree Sparrows may raise up to three broods in a year, although smaller boxes tend to hold fewer consecutive broods in any one year. Do not be tempted to remove the foul-looking nest after a brood has fledged as this will cause the parents to nest elsewhere. Only clean boxes after the protracted nesting season is over in late September or October.

	Jan	Feb	Mar	Apr	May	Jun	Jul	Aug	Sep	Oct	Nov	Dec
Egg laying												
Incubation												
Nestlings												

Pied Flycatcher — *Ficedula hypoleuca*

Nestbox	Small hole-entrance box, 28 mm diameter hole
Distribution/ status	Wales and western England, scarce elsewhere. Green
Siting	Woodland, preferably overlooking a glade. 2 m – 4 m high
Nest	A large cup of leaves, grass, bark, moss and lichen lined with hair, grass and possibly wool or feathers
Eggs	5–8; pale blue
Density	Boxes can be as close as 25 m apart, territory size 0.2 hectares in optimal habitat
Incubation	12–13 days, by female
Nestling	14–16 days
Broods	1

The Pied Flycatcher is locally abundant over much of western Britain and is found, typically, in oak woodland. It may be absent from apparently suitable areas simply because of a lack of nest sites. By the time this summer visitor arrives, prime nesting holes have often been commandeered by the resident tits. This situation has become worse with the warming of the British climate because resident tits now nest even earlier. Pied Flycatchers often take very readily to nestboxes and in some places populations are dependent on the provision of nestboxes.

Set the box at medium height (from 2 to 4 m), preferably overlooking a woodland glade or in a wood with little natural undergrowth. Ensure there is a suitable branch for perching within a couple of metres of the box and that there is a clear approach to the box.

If competition with tits is a problem, boxes can be mounted in small clusters. Tits will not nest very close to each other, leaving some boxes free for Pied Flycatchers. Alternatively, holes may be blocked with a cork until the flycatchers arrive, by which time most of the tits will already be using other holes. (Remember to check that the box has no occupants before blocking the hole.)

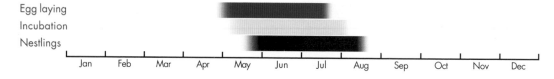

	Jan	Feb	Mar	Apr	May	Jun	Jul	Aug	Sep	Oct	Nov	Dec
Egg laying												
Incubation												
Nestlings												

Nuthatch — *Sitta europaea*

Nestbox	Small hole-entrance box, 32 mm diameter hole
Distribution/ status	England and Wales but absent from much of Cumbria and East Midlands. Green
Siting	Above 3 m if possible with clear flight path to nest entrance
Nest	Mud plastered around the entrance, sides and roof of the nest cavity. The floor is lined with wood chippings and leaves
Eggs	6–9; white, variably speckled reddish
Density	1 box per hectare
Incubation	14–15 days, by female
Nestling	23–25 days
Broods	1 (2)

The Nuthatch is present throughout much of England and Wales but is highly sedentary and may not colonise apparently suitable places unless there are nearby populations producing surplus birds. Although it is primarily a bird of mature broad-leafed woodland, it will live happily in parkland and suburban areas where there are sufficient trees. It is absent from areas of intensive arable agriculture, such as in parts of Lincolnshire, where there are few wooded places.

Nuthatches will nest in standard small hole boxes, although they will also quite happily use larger cavities. They plaster mud around the entrance hole to ensure that it is only just big enough for them to enter. This helps exclude larger birds, such as Starlings, from otherwise suitable nesting holes.

If Nuthatches use nestboxes, they usually plaster mud under the lid to seal any gaps. When inspecting boxes in the nesting season, take great care not to let this dried mud fall from under the lid on to the eggs or nestlings below.

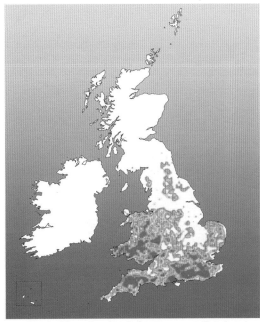

Nuthatch is mainly a bird of mature woodland and is common only in southern England and Wales.
(From *The New Atlas of Breeding Birds in Britain and Ireland: 1988–91*)

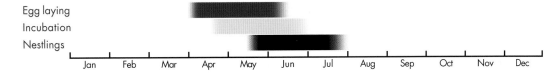

	Jan	Feb	Mar	Apr	May	Jun	Jul	Aug	Sep	Oct	Nov	Dec
Egg laying												
Incubation												
Nestlings												

Redstart – *Phoenicurus phoenicurus*

Nestbox	Small hole-entrance box, 40 mm diameter hole
Distribution/ status	Rare or absent in East Anglia, Midlands, Home Counties. Absent from Ireland. Amber
Siting	On trees at 1 m – 3 m high in or near woodland or parkland
Nest	Dead grass, moss, roots or bark lined with hair and feathers
Eggs	5–7; light blue
Density	Territory from 1 hectare
Incubation	13–14 days, by female
Nestling	14–16 days
Broods	1–2

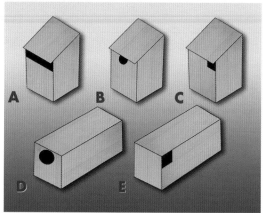

Redstarts have taken to a variety of designs of nestboxes, but seem to have specific local preferences. The common features of these boxes used are that they are larger than normal tit boxes, with a larger entrance hole and a darker nesting chamber. If Redstarts are present in your area but they do not take to the standard hole entrance boxes put out for them, try a different design. The picture (right) shows a variety of successful designs.

In order to provide a darker nesting cavity, particularly in an open-fronted design, an inner chamber can be constructed using a partition part-way across the inside of the box. For hole entrance boxes, a hole in one corner of the front, rather than centrally placed, can give a darker nesting area in the opposite corner. A narrow landing ledge below the hole may also be of assistance.

Site the box at between 1 m and 3 m high in large gardens with mature trees or on the edge of woodland, preferably on an oak and also ensure there are plenty of song posts nearby. Redstarts suffer from competition from other hole nesting birds and so the challenge is to find a design that Redstarts are happy with but that the competition (Pied Flycatchers, Blue Tits etc.) do not like. Redstarts are sensitive to disturbance and boxes should be sited away from well-used footpaths or other areas which are often frequented by humans.

Alternative designs for Redstarts. A, B & C have bases 175 mm square and fronts 200 mm high. D & E are 300 mm long with cross section of 125 mm. A: Open-fronted, 40 mm gap between front and roof; B: hole diameter 40 mm; C: 40 mm square hole at one side of front; D: Long box, 40 mm diameter entrance at one end. E: Long box, 40 mm square entrance at end of one side.

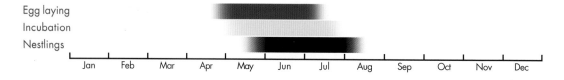

Egg laying
Incubation
Nestlings

Jan Feb Mar Apr May Jun Jul Aug Sep Oct Nov Dec

Medium hole-entrance nestboxes

Starling
Great Spotted Woodpecker

Exploded view

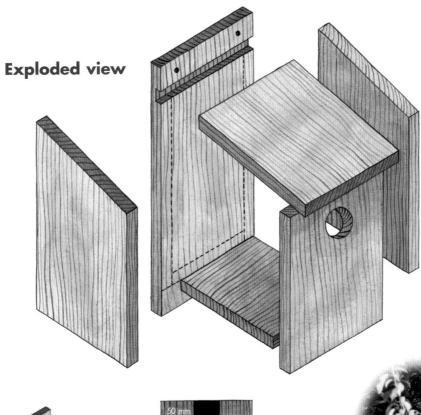

Front of box with
square entrance hole

Front of box with
triangular entrance hole

Alternative hole entrance shapes for ease of cutting

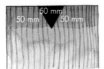

Medium hole-entrance nestboxes

Construction
Medium hole-entrance boxes are similar to the small hole design but, because of their larger size, will be heavier. Some design features will therefore become relatively more important. Nails and mounting methods will need to be stronger and more care must be taken to ensure safety of the tree, box and nestboxer when siting these boxes.

Drainage
Drainage is important. Even if the joints of the floor are not watertight, the wood may swell in wet weather preventing water from draining out. To avoid this, drill 5 holes of 3 mm diameter in the box base.

Entrance size and shape
If you are making only a handful of these boxes and the expense of a hole saw or large wood twist bit is not justified, the round hole can be substituted with a square or triangular hole cut in the top of the box front using a saw. A hole 45 mm square will give access to both Starlings and Great Spotted Woodpeckers.

Materials and cutting diagram
The cutting diagram gives dimensions for a typical medium box made from a single rough-cut timber plank. Using exterior-quality plywood sheeting instead will produce lighter boxes and may allow dimensions to be altered more easily to suit particular circumstances.

Filled boxes
As Great Spotted Woodpeckers need to excavate their own nesting cavity, boxes must be stuffed with suitable material such as birch taken from a dead, fallen tree, soft enough to be sliced with a knife in order to fit snugly inside the box. Alternatively, expanded polystyrene blocks can be used for stuffing. (For the sake of the environment, use only discarded polystyrene.)

Other species
Although these boxes are not intended for smaller birds, do not be surprised if other species, such as Great Tits, use them.

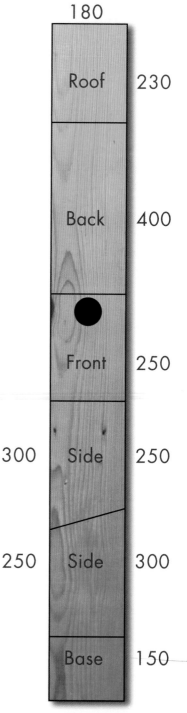

180

Roof	230
Back	400
Front	250

300 | Side | 250

250 | Side | 300

| Base | 150 |

Plank size
180 mm x 1580 mm
(All dimensions in millimetres)

Starling — *Sturnus vulgaris*

Nestbox	Medium hole-entrance box, 45 mm diameter hole
Distribution/ status	Present everywhere except remote mountainous areas. Red
Siting	Height above 2·5 m on tree trunks or buildings
Nest	A heap of plant material, lined with feathers, moss and wool. In traditional sites the nest may be many layers deep
Eggs	4–7; light blue
Density	Can nest colonially; boxes may be in adjacent trees or close together on buildings
Incubation	12–14 days, by both sexes
Nestling	20–22 days
Broods	1–2

CBC/BBS population index (England)

The British breeding population of Starlings has declined by over 50% in the last 25 years and the species is now on the Red List. The apparent abundance of the species on farmland and in gardens in winter is due to an influx of migrant birds from north-eastern Europe. In spite of their aggressive behaviour and association with mankind, Starlings are sensitive to disturbance at the nest.

Starlings will nest at any height where there is a suitable cavity but prefer higher sites and so boxes should placed at 2.5 m or higher. Because of their gregarious nature they will happily nest near to each other so several boxes may be placed close together — on adjacent trees for instance. Make sure there is a clear, direct flight path to the nest entrance. Boxes placed on balconies of high-rise buildings could be used by Starlings.

The nest is usually an untidy layer of dried grass lined with fur, moss or feathers. The fresh green leaves which they add to the nest before laying eggs deter parasites. Starlings

may rear a second brood in the same nest site with little additional nest building on top of the old and will often re-use the site year after year, adding new material to the previous years' decaying nest. To prevent this unhealthy accumulation of material, boxes should be cleaned at the end of the season after the second brood has fledged.

Single Starling eggs are often found apparently abandoned below an active nest. This is likely to be a result of a female laying an egg in the nest of another Starling pair and the owners rejecting it.

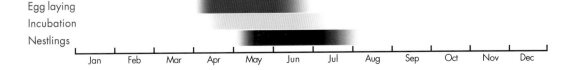

Egg laying											
Incubation											
Nestlings											
Jan	Feb	Mar	Apr	May	Jun	Jul	Aug	Sep	Oct	Nov	Dec

Great Spotted Woodpecker –
Dendrocopos major

Nestbox	Medium hole-entrance box, 50 mm diameter hole, filled with soft wood or polystyrene
Distribution/ status	Absent only from Ireland and treeless parts of Scottish Highlands. Green
Siting	3 m – 5 m on tree trunk
Nest	No lining material added to cavity
Eggs	4–7; white
Density	1 box per 2 hectares in optimal habitats
Incubation	12–18 days, by both sexes
Nestling	18–21 days
Broods	1

Great Spotted Woodpeckers are generally creatures of parkland and woodland although their population is increasing steadily and they can be frequent visitors to garden bird feeding stations. They do not often nest in boxes but they are well worth trying to attract.

These woodpeckers will nest in a medium-sized box but it needs to be stuffed with a soft material for them to excavate their own nesting cavity. Fill the entire box except for a small indentation behind the entrance. This will simulate a natural wound in a tree trunk and signal a weak spot where hole boring will be easier to start.

Boxes should be placed on a tree trunk at least 3 m above ground level. Ensure the box is in a secluded place, with an unobstructed flight path.

A rotten piece of birch log provides the stuffing for this woodpecker box.

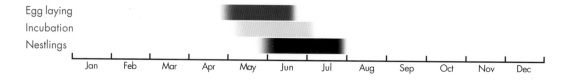

	Jan	Feb	Mar	Apr	May	Jun	Jul	Aug	Sep	Oct	Nov	Dec
Egg laying												
Incubation												
Nestlings												

Jackdaw
Stock Dove
Tawny Owl

Exploded view

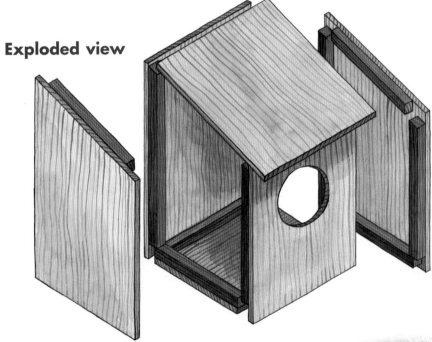

A large box with a sideways-projecting dowel to be used as a perch by adults and fledgling young

Large hole-entrance nestboxes

Materials

Large boxes can be made from wide rough-cut timber planks but these can be very expensive. In addition, boxes made from planks are very heavy, difficult to handle and require very strong mounting arrangements. An effective alternative is exterior-quality plywood, which can be bought in sheets but can often be found discarded after initial use. Boxes made with this material should have an inner supporting framework of 25 mm square battens.

Other sources of materials

Various ready-made timber packing cases or barrels can be adapted easily although you may need to weatherproof them using roofing felt. Hardboard, thin plywood and chipboard will deteriorate quickly when exposed to weather. Do not make boxes of these materials unless they are to be sited within buildings.

Entrance

The hole needs to be larger than can be cut by commonly-used wood-boring equipment. A circular hole is not important so an entrance is most conveniently made by cutting a rectangle from the top of the box front. Alternatively a rounded hole can be cut with a jig-saw.

Drainage

Drainage holes are very important — bore nine holes of 5 mm diameter in the base of the box.

Preparing the nest

Most larger species prefer the nestbox to have a layer of loose dry material over the floor. The best material is chopped dry bark (dead twigs and small branches fed through a garden shredder will be ideal) but shavings can be used instead. Peat and other softer materials should not be used because they tend to retain moisture and heat up as they decompose.

Location

Large boxes can be very obvious so do not site them in places where they are likely to be the target of vandals or other unwanted human attention. In urban areas, for example, boxes could be sited high on buildings.

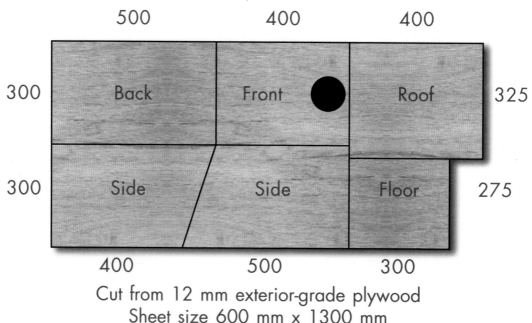

Cut from 12 mm exterior-grade plywood
Sheet size 600 mm x 1300 mm

(All dimensions in millimetres)

Jackdaw — *Corvus monedula*

Nestbox	Large hole-entrance box, 150 mm diameter hole
Distribution/ status	Absent only from parts of western Scotland. Green
Siting	At least 3 m high, but as high as possible in buildings or trees
Nest	Sticks, lined with wool, hair or various other materials. In small holes there may be no twigs
Eggs	4–6; pale blue with some darker speckles
Density	May nest colonially, boxes can be placed close together
Incubation	17–18 days, by female
Nestling	30–35 days
Broods	1

Jackdaws will nest in cavities at any height but seem to be more comfortable at greater heights. Nests have been recorded as high as 70 m on towers but boxes placed as low as 3 m can be successful.

The size of the Jackdaw nest depends on the size of the nesting cavity. The birds will continue adding twigs to the base of the nest until the accumulated heap reaches the desired height. Thus, providing a bigger box may only force the adults to collect more material. One Jackdaw nest on record consisted of a pile of twigs 3 m deep.

Jackdaws are sensitive to disturbance and need a flight path to the nest which is free of obstructions and away from constant human activity. They are gregarious birds — they can often be seen nesting in adjacent chimney pots — so boxes may be placed close together. In spite of their sensitivity, they frequently select nesting sites in cavities in buildings. Boxes built into loft spaces with an entrance through a gable end wall can be productive nesting places for this species.

A built-in Jackdaw nestbox in the roof-space.

Jackdaw nest after young have fledged. Note the variety of materials used for lining the nest including moss, hair, straw and litter.

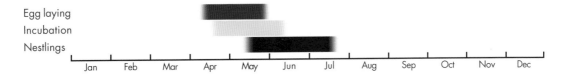

Egg laying
Incubation
Nestlings

Jan Feb Mar Apr May Jun Jul Aug Sep Oct Nov Dec

Stock Dove — *Columba oenas*

Nestbox	Large hole-entrance box, 150 mm diameter hole
Distribution/ status	Widespread in England, Wales, southern Scotland and southeast Ireland. Amber
Siting	At least 3 m high. Best location on edge of woodland overlooking open fields
Nest	A thin layer of twigs, roots and other debris. A deep layer of droppings will accumulate during the season
Eggs	1–3; plain white
Density	May nest semi-colonially. Increase number of boxes until no more are used
Incubation	16–18 days, by both sexes
Nestling	24–28 days
Broods	2–5

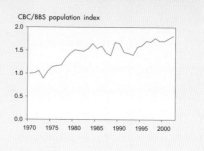

CBC/BBS population index

The Stock Dove population is recovering following a decline in the 1950s and 1960s resulting from a reduction in productivity caused by organochlorine seed dressings.

Unlike many other pigeons, Stock Doves nest in cavities and take readily to nestboxes. The best sites for boxes are those near to, or overlooking, open fields. Boxes can be sited on trees or outbuildings, but Stock Doves will also nest in cavities within large open sheds or barns. The flight path should allow an approach to the nest which is clear of frequent human activity. A landing platform at the nest entrance, or a convenient branch

nearby, is helpful but not essential. Ivy growing near the box or on it, may help to attract them.

Stock Dove nests often suffer from predation by Tawny Owls or grey squirrels but the long breeding season with multiple attempts usually ensures that some young survive. Up to five successive broods have been recorded from a pair within a single year. The next clutch of eggs may be laid before the preceding brood leaves the nest. Droppings, which the adults do not clear from the nest, may foul these eggs and prevent them from hatching. If boxes are placed on adjacent trees, a pair of Stock Doves can rear alternate broods in the two boxes, allowing one nest to dry out while the other is in use. Clean out the box at the end of the season (which may be in October or even November), leaving a fresh lining of wood bark or chippings for next season. The year's accumulated layer of droppings is excellent for the compost heap.

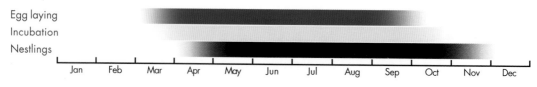

Egg laying
Incubation
Nestlings

Jan Feb Mar Apr May Jun Jul Aug Sep Oct Nov Dec

Tawny Owl – *Strix aluco*

Nestbox	Large hole-entrance box, 150 mm diameter hole
Distribution/ status	Widespread in mainland UK, absent from Ireland. Green
Siting	At least 2·5 m high on a tree Ensure there is a clear flight path to the box
Nest	No material added but a scrape may be made in the base of the cavity
Eggs	2–5; white
Density	1 box per 20 hectares
Incubation	28–30 days, by female
Nestling	32–35 days
Broods	1

Although Tawny Owls are primarily birds of deciduous woodland, they are not uncommon in villages and towns, and even in the greener parts of cities. They nest readily in boxes, particularly in habitats such as young woodland plantations, where there is adequate food but no large nesting holes in trees.

The height of the nest is of little importance to the owls provided the box is free of disturbance, particularly by humans, although it is unlikely that a site below 3 m would be suitable.

Like other large birds, they drop from the nest site in order to gain flying speed — so ensure the flight path is clear, particularly below the front of the box. A perch made of a 25 mm diameter dowel or a branch projecting from the side of the box is helpful.

Boxes are best sited during the winter in Tawny Owl territories. These territories can be located by visiting during the night in December and listening for calling owls.

Tawny Owls are sensitive to disturbance, particularly early in the season, and can be dangerous if approached. Eyes are a particular target for attack by their talons. They are best left alone during the breeding season.

Unlike many other hole-nesting birds, Tawny Owl chicks leave the nest before they are able to fly freely and spend some days scrambling amongst nearby branches. They are sometimes found, apparently helpless, on the ground. In these cases it is best to place the chick as high as you can reach in

This fledgling is too young to fly but has already left the nest and is climbing freely about the tree.

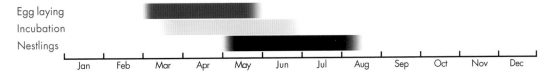

	Jan	Feb	Mar	Apr	May	Jun	Jul	Aug	Sep	Oct	Nov	Dec
Egg laying												
Incubation												
Nestlings												

the nearest bush, well out of the way of dogs and children. You should never assume it has been abandoned and is in need of human foster parents. When siting boxes, ensure that there are adequate branches and other footholds nearby which the flightless young can utilise to move around.

When cleaning the boxes after the owls have fledged, it is always worth examining the prey remains in the nest in order to record the small mammal fauna and, sometimes, recover bird rings.

Any bird rings found should be reported to the BTO through the website *www.bto.org/ringing/ ringinfo/foundring.htm* or to The Ringing Unit, BTO, The Nunnery, Thetford, Norfolk, IP24 2PU, giving details of ring number, date, place and circumstances of recovery.

Tawny Owl nest with two downy nestlings and the third nestling chipping at the egg. Also present are two dead wood mice in the 'larder'.

The chimney style of box, with entrance at the top end, is preferred by Tawny Owls in some areas.

Tawny Owl pellets — remains of bird feathers can be seen in the pellet on the left.

Two developing Tawny Owl nestlings, safe and dry in a well-built owl box.

Swift

Exploded view

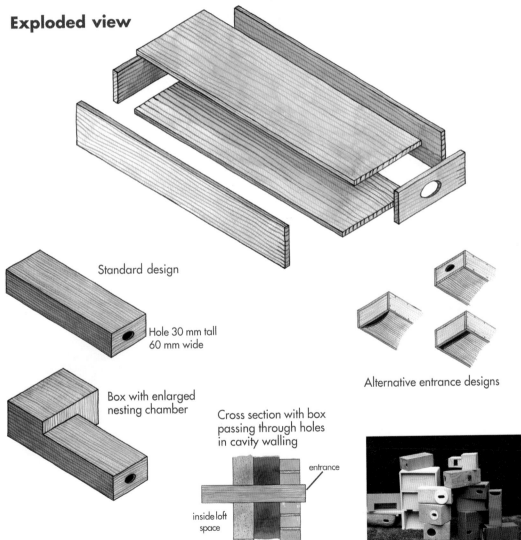

Standard design

Hole 30 mm tall
60 mm wide

Box with enlarged
nesting chamber

Cross section with box
passing through holes
in cavity walling

entrance

inside loft
space

Alternative entrance designs

Swifts will use a wide range of
box designs

Swift — *Apus apus*

Nestbox	Hole-entrance special design
Distribution/ status	Scarce or absent in northwest Scotland only. Green
Siting	As high as possible on buildings with a clear drop below entrance
Nest	A cup of plant material collected on the wing and cemented with saliva
Eggs	2–3; dull white
Density	Colonial nester, as many boxes as can be conveniently sited
Incubation	18–20 days, by both sexes
Nestling	35–36 days
Broods	1

Swifts spend most of their time on the wing, rarely coming to land except for nesting. There is some evidence to suggest that our British breeding population is declining, possibly because of a lack of suitable nesting sites as older buildings with suitable nesting holes are demolished or renovated.

Site boxes as high as possible, under the eaves of a house or within a loft with just the entrance hole protruding through the wall. The exact shape and size of the box is not important — Swifts can nest in very confined spaces. However, if it is possible within the constraints of the roof space, make the nesting chamber at the far end of the box wider and a little higher than the tunnel of the box. A ring of plaited straw placed at the back end of the box to act as a base for the nest may help to attract Swifts. Nests of this species may contain many large parasites which over-winter, waiting to infest next year's nest inhabitants. Clean the boxes once the Swifts have departed in September or October.

The design depicted is for installation within the roof space of a building. It projects through a hole in the brickwork and can rest on the bricks of the inner and outer walls. For single brick walls, additional supporting brackets may be needed inside the building. The box can be built of lighter grade plywood than that used to construct boxes exposed to the elements, providing that the entrance is sheltered above by overhanging eaves. The cross section of the box will need to be altered depending on the size of bricks in the walls.

The diagrams show an entrance hole, at least 30 mm tall and 60 mm wide, in the end of the box. This type of entrance can also be used by other species, such as House

Swift nestling with an unhatched egg.

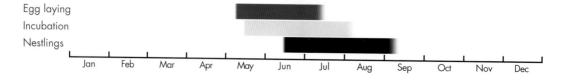

Egg laying

Incubation

Nestlings

Jan   Feb   Mar   Apr   May   Jun   Jul   Aug   Sep   Oct   Nov   Dec

Sparrows or Starlings. If competition for nesting holes with these species is a problem, the entrance may be made in the underside of the box. Boxes with entrances in the underside must protrude from the wall of the house. (If competition is a problem ensure there are other boxes for the competing species.)

If boxes are placed in areas where former Swift nest sites have been destroyed, nestboxes may be found and used immediately. In other places, it may be some years before they are colonised — be patient. Swifts are sensitive to disturbance so inspect and record events in their nests with great care.

Some roof tiles with integral Swift boxes are now available. It is easier to include these when the house is being built or re-tiled, than afterwards.

Boxes may also be hung under the eaves of buildings. Such boxes must be made from

A roomier built-in box. Inspection is through the opening side. (The hole at the inner end is for photography.) Note the wire support on the top of the box.

weatherproof materials. Suitable boxes are produced commercially.

Swifts can nest colonially so, if space allows, place several boxes close together in or on the same building.

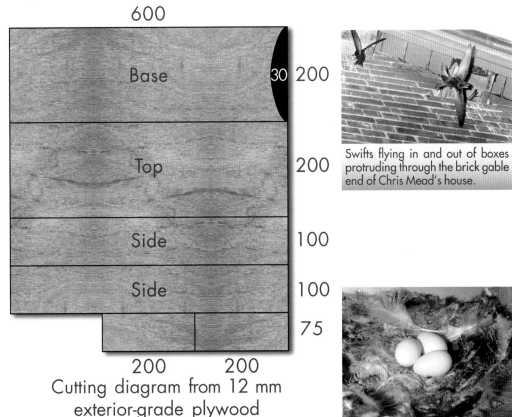

600

Base 30 200

Top 200

Swifts flying in and out of boxes protruding through the brick gable end of Chris Mead's house.

Side 100

Side 100

75

200 200

Cutting diagram from 12 mm exterior-grade plywood

(All dimensions in millimetres)

A large Swift clutch of three eggs.

Special hole-entrance nestboxes

Barn Owl

Exploded view

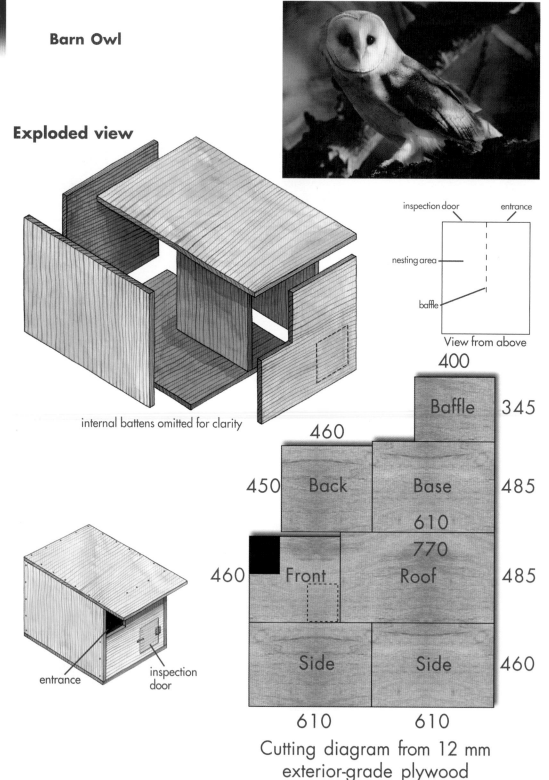

internal battens omitted for clarity

inspection door · entrance

nesting area

baffle

View from above

entrance · inspection door

400

Baffle · 345

460

450 · Back

Base · 485

610

770

460 · Front

Roof · 485

Side · Side · 460

610 · 610

Cutting diagram from 12 mm exterior-grade plywood

(All dimensions in millimetres)

Barn Owl – *Tyto alba*

Nestbox	Hole-entrance special design. At least 450 mm wide, 450 mm high and 750 mm deep. Entrance at least 150 mm wide by 200 mm high
Distribution/ status	Widespread but local in Wales, central and southern England; increasingly scarce elsewhere. Amber
Siting	Away from roads, clear, undisturbed flight path to nest entrance, at least 4 m high
Nest	None, or a hollow in the floor of the cavity
Eggs	4–7; white
Density	Territory size from 60 hectares
Incubation	32–34 days, by female.
Nestling	56–75 days
Broods	1–2

Population Estimates

1932 = 12,000
(England and Wales) (Blaker)

1982–85 = 4,400
(Britain) (Hawk Trust)

1995–97 = 4,000
(UK) (The Hawk & Owl Trust/BTO)

The Barn Owl is a Schedule 1 species which means that it is against the law to inspect active Barn Owl nests without possessing the necessary licence. Barn Owl populations have decreased greatly for a variety of reasons including loss of nesting sites. Provision of boxes therefore can help ameliorate their problems.

There is no limit to the size of box which will suit Barn Owls: the bigger the better. The entrance hole should be situated at least half way up the front of the box to reduce the chance of premature departure by the young. Boxes should have an interior baffle running $^1/_2$ to $^3/_4$ of the distance from front to back and reaching $^3/_4$ of the way to the roof. This partition gives extra seclusion and shelter to the birds whilst still allowing adequate ventilation in the nesting chamber. The cutting diagram gives a design which can be made from a standard 2,440 mm x 1,220 mm sheet of exterior grade plywood. Boxes sited

outside may require additional weatherproofing with roofing felt.

Boxes may be sited inside buildings, in trees, on poles or in straw stacks. Boxes for use in buildings or in trees are described below, but for other designs consult the Hawk & Owl Trust **(see Appendix)**. Barn Owls require

A tea chest, used for nesting Barn Owls, mounted securely on roof timbers in an old barn.

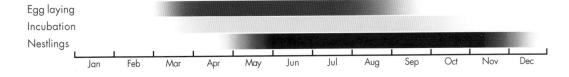

Egg laying												
Incubation												
Nestlings												
	Jan	Feb	Mar	Apr	May	Jun	Jul	Aug	Sep	Oct	Nov	Dec

both nesting and roosting sites so siting two boxes in each territory will be helpful.

In buildings — Almost any large box, tea chest or packing case, can be converted into a box which should be fixed to a wall or beam by strong brackets. If the box is on a beam ensure cats cannot reach it — thorny twigs tied to the beam can help keep them off. Alternatively a whole section of the gable end of a floored loft can be blocked off from the main building leaving an 'owl loft'. If the box is in a building used for storing foodstuffs, ensure that the birds cannot contaminate the foods. This can be done by siting the box with its entrance abutting the entrance hole in the wall of the building.

Conversion of agricultural buildings into housing often leads to loss of nest sites. This loss can be prevented if Barn Owl nesting sites are retained when conversions are made. If engaging in a house conversion or extension (provided the surrounding habitat is suitable), consider whether a Barn Owl box can be incorporated into the loft space of the building.

In trees — Barn Owls frequently nest in large tree holes. Isolated tall broken stumps are often very suitable sites for boxes. Boxes in

Barn Owls will readily nest in old hollow tree trunks.

trees must be thoroughly weatherproofed and face southeast, away from prevailing winds.

Barn Owls are sensitive to disturbance at all times, so boxes should be sited in quiet locations. The owls must have constant access to the box so a hole in a wall is better than leaving a window or door open. Boxes should be sited in locations away from busy roads because Barn Owls hunting along roadside verges are very vulnerable to collision with traffic. Boxes are best put up on the edge of existing Barn Owl strongholds — local knowledge will be useful here. The height of boxes is of little importance to the owls themselves, the main considerations being the possibility of interference by humans and predation. A typical minimum workable height is about 3 m. Boxes should be cleaned every year or two, leaving just a thin layer of pellets over the floor and new boxes should be lined with bark chippings.

A large, healthy brood of nestlings reared in an old packing case.

Small open-fronted nestboxes

Robin

Pied Wagtail

Wren

Spotted Flycatcher

Exploded view

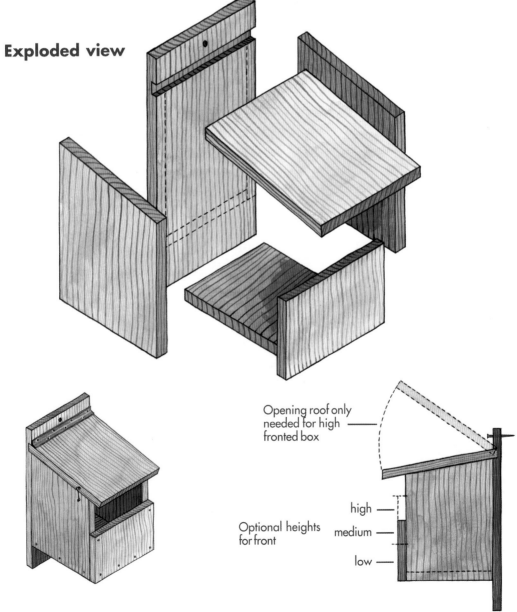

Opening roof only
needed for high
fronted box

Optional heights
for front

high

medium

low

Small open-fronted nestboxes

Front entrance

The open-fronted nestbox is identical to a hole entrance box except that the upper part of the front is cut away. The cutting diagram shows three choices for the front panel. The standard design, which will attract the widest variety of species, uses the medium sized front (100 mm). The high or low fronted designs will attract fewer species but are much more suitable for their target species (Wren and Spotted Flycatcher respectively). Details of these are given in the species sections.

Roof

Because the access hole is so large there is generally no need for the complications of an inspection hatch and so roofs can be nailed or screwed on. Only boxes with the high front, and hence a very narrow entrance, should have an opening roof for easy inspection and cleaning. As with hole-entrance boxes, roofs should overhang the front to provide shelter.

Traditionally, small boxes have been made with a sloping roof from back down to front. Less pleasing to the eye, rather more awkward to construct but possibly a little better in the rain, are roofs sloping to one side. Rain draining from the roof will then run off of the side of the box rather than in front of the open entrance.

Location

Open-fronted boxes are more vulnerable to predators than are hole entrance boxes and care must be taken when siting these boxes to minimise accessibility to predators. This can be achieved by hiding boxes in thorny bushes, by mounting boxes on sheer faces such as house walls, or by shielding the front of the box with a wire mesh guard. Some species, such as Robins, nest in sites well hidden from human view. Others, such as Spotted Flycatchers, prefer an open site where the sitting bird has a good view of the surrounding area. Such specific requirements must be taken into account when siting boxes.

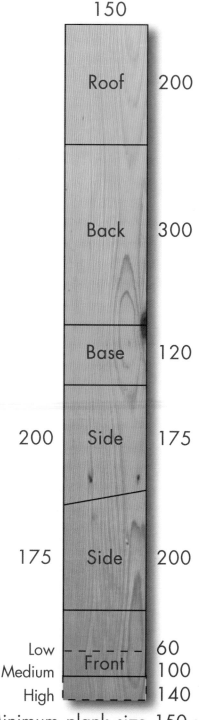

Minimum plank size 150 x 1095 mm (for medium height front)

(All dimensions in millimetres)

Robin — *Erithacus rubecula*

Nestbox	Small open-fronted nestbox. Front 100 mm high
Distribution/ status	Present everywhere. Green status
Siting	Well hidden by thick overhanging vegetation. Can be low if cats are not a problem
Nest	A large cup of leaves, grass and moss lined with roots or hairs. The nest may be domed when built in some enclosed spaces
Eggs	5–7; white with a variable amount of speckles
Density	Territory size from 0.5 hectares
Incubation	12–14 days, by female
Nestling	12–15 days
Broods	2 (3)

The nests of Robins are amongst the hardest to find of small British birds and for this reason it is best to place boxes for them in well concealed sites. There is no need for a clear flight path to the nest as the birds will happily hop into the box. Open nests are more vulnerable to predation than those in holes and this may explain why the brightly coloured Robin prefers such well-hidden sites.

Boxes may be sited at any height up to about 5 m but, overall, height is less important than concealment. Boxes may be hidden under the overhanging vegetation of a ditch or embankment, wedged in a fork deep in a thorny bush or hedge, hidden behind thick ivy on a tree or behind a creeper on a wall or fence.

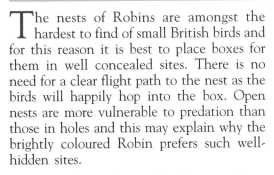

Robins have two or more broods in a season and successive broods may all be raised in the same site.

An alternative design which is also very suitable for Robins is a small hole entrance box with a 65 mm diameter hole. Robins are often depicted as nesting in discarded man-made artefacts such as teapots or kettles. Although these may be more suitable than no site at all, they provide less insulation and are more subject to condensation than wooden boxes.

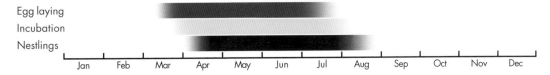

	Jan	Feb	Mar	Apr	May	Jun	Jul	Aug	Sep	Oct	Nov	Dec
Egg laying												
Incubation												
Nestlings												

Pied Wagtail — *Motacilla alba*

Nestbox	Small open-fronted box, medium (100 mm) front
Distribution/ status	Present everywhere. Green
Siting	Up to 5 m high, sites near grass and water may be preferred, can be located on human artefacts
Nest	Twigs, roots and moss, lined with locally available material
Eggs	5–8; greyish, speckled brown
Density	Territories from 5 hectares but may nest much more closely in very good habitats (e.g. sewage farms)
Incubation	12–13 days, by both sexes
Nestling	14–16 days
Broods	2 (3)

Pied Wagtails take to artificial sites very readily. Their nests may be found on ledges in buildings, in piles of wood or stone, in unused drainpipes, on structures built of metal girders, in holes in walls, on machinery in farm outbuildings or under bridges. Habitats which have some water (ponds, streams, sewage beds) and some stretches of open grass are most suitable for this species.

Pied Wagtails may nest at any height from ground level upwards but typically boxes should be sited between 1 m and 5 m above ground level. Alternatively boxes may be attached to external girders on roofs of buildings.

Because Pied Wagtails take to such a variety of artificial nest sites, there is no need to adhere slavishly to any particular design. Many small wooden packing boxes can be adapted easily to make suitable nestboxes for them. Simply ensure that there is a nesting cavity at least as large as in the standard nestbox design and the entrance hole is at least 50 mm by 50 mm.

Long box with entrance at one end, giving a secluded nesting area at the other end, attached to girders above a building.

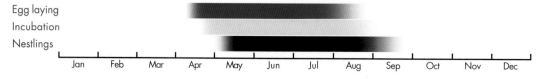

	Jan	Feb	Mar	Apr	May	Jun	Jul	Aug	Sep	Oct	Nov	Dec
Egg laying												
Incubation												
Nestlings												

Wren — *Troglodytes troglodytes*

Nestbox	Small open-fronted box, high (140 mm) front
Distribution/ status	Present everywhere. Green
Siting	Well hidden, preferably in thick, thorny undergrowth. Clear flight path to nest not needed
Nest	A domed structure of leaves, moss and grass
Eggs	5–6; white
Density	Territory size from 0.5 hectares upwards. Clusters of 2 or 3 boxes will cater for successive broods by same pair
Incubation	14–15 days, by female
Nestling	16–17 days
Broods	2 (3)

Wrens often nest in cavities from ground level up to a height of about 5 m. Boxes should be well hidden by vegetation, preferably prickly or thorny species such as *Berberis*, or gorse which give extra protection against predators. Brambles are frequently used by Wrens and boxes wedged in the larger, woody stems in a bramble clump may be successful.

Although Wrens will take to larger sized boxes, there is little point in making them. The nest chamber in the centre of the nest will be about the same size whatever the dimensions of the nestbox. Provision of bigger boxes will only give the adult Wrens more work in the collection of nesting material.

The male Wren will build several unlined 'cock nests', before the female selects one and lines it with feathers. If you find a cock nest in your box, it is worth putting up two or three more boxes in similar sites a few metres from the first. The male is fairly likely to select one of these for a later nest since he is already a box user. At the end of the season you might wish to remove all but one of these boxes in order to have a supply of spares ready for the next season. Do not empty boxes of unused 'cock nests' until the end of August as the female may still use one of these for a late brood even if it has been standing empty for several weeks or even months.

Often, close inspection of the interior of a 'wild' Wren nest is not possible without damaging the nest structure. However, those in boxes with an opening lid can often be inspected, with care, as the box holds the nest inside together.

Wrens will also use small hole entrance boxes, usually with a hole diameter of 28 mm or more. Placing such a box in a well hidden site will allow the Wren to use it and discourage other species, such as tits or sparrows, which need a clear flight path to the nest.

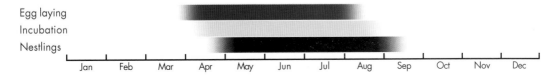

	Jan	Feb	Mar	Apr	May	Jun	Jul	Aug	Sep	Oct	Nov	Dec
Egg laying												
Incubation												
Nestlings												

Spotted Flycatcher — *Muscicapa striata*

Nestbox	Small open-fronted box, low (60 mm) front
Distribution/ status	Widespread, becoming scarcer in northwest UK. Red
Siting	2 m – 4 m with clear outlook over grass with scattered trees
Nest	A tiny cup of miscellaneous material including spiders' webs, lined with feathers and leaves
Eggs	4–5; off-white, usually mottled reddish
Density	1 box per hectare
Incubation	12–14 days, mostly by female
Nestling	12–15 days
Broods	1–2

CBC/BBS population index

Spotted Flycatchers prefer a nest site with a clear outlook but with shelter above. The area in front of the box should be open — a large lawn or woodland glade is ideal. Overhanging leaves may obscure the box from the outside world but still allow the sitting bird a good view, and so creepers growing on house walls often provide ideal nesting sites. Spotted Flycatchers may nest at any height from almost ground level to 10 m but typically a box should be placed between 2 m and 4 m from the ground.

Spotted Flycatchers hunt by watching potential flying insect prey from a perch, then chasing the target on the wing, performing their characteristic aerobatic flight. Once the prey has been caught the bird returns to the perch, before moving on to the nest. It is therefore necessary to ensure the nest site has suitable perching sites nearby — even sticks pushed into the ground will do.

The function of their nestbox is twofold — to provide shelter from above and to stop the nest from falling out. There are many other artificial sites which provide these conditions. A missing brick in an old wall would provide a sheltered cavity and a small wooden batten placed along the front of the hole can ensure any nest will not fall to the ground. Ideally the missing brick should be screened by vegetation.

If there is no suitable vegetation to screen nest sites, boxes can be protected to some extent by placing a 30 cm diameter hemisphere of 50 mm chicken wire over the front of the box. This will prevent larger avian and mammalian predators from reaching the eggs or chicks.

Egg laying											
Incubation											
Nestlings											
Jan	Feb	Mar	Apr	May	Jun	Jul	Aug	Sep	Oct	Nov	Dec

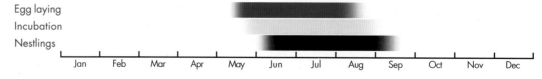

Large open-fronted nestboxes

Kestrel

Exploded view

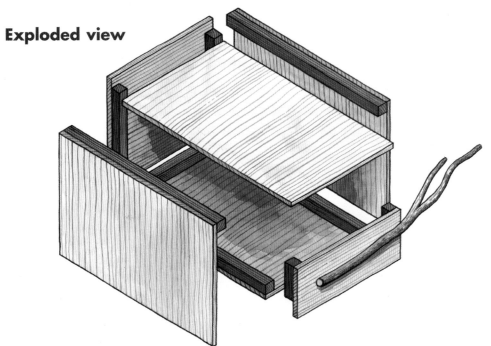

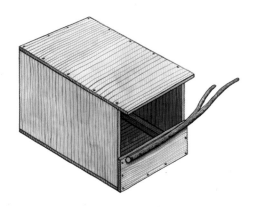

The wooden board is used to attach heavy boxes securely to trees or to buildings.

Large open-fronted nestboxes

This box is designed primarily to attract Kestrels, although other species including Stock Doves, Jackdaws and Tawny Owls may sometimes use it.

Construction

The advice on construction and location is the same as for large hole-entrance boxes. Avoid thin, man-made materials (except exterior plywood). Various ready-made boxes and packing cases can be adapted, but these will need to have half of one end cut away for the entrance. The mounting method must be very strong and secure. The cutting diagram given below is for use with a sheet of exterior quality plywood. A perch is required and is best made of a broomstick-thick branch which bends upwards at an angle to the side.

Mounting

The box is best mounted so the floor slopes slightly backwards. This will prevent eggs from rolling away from the nest, which is normally made in the back of the box where it is darkest.

Drainage and waterproofing

The large open front is likely to allow some rainwater into the front of the box so ensure any such water can drain away by boring a few small holes in the floor of the box. Boxes will last longer and be much more weatherproof if the top is covered with roofing felt.

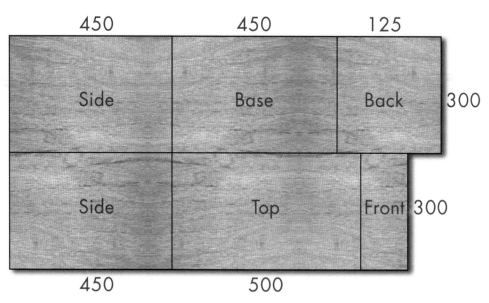

Adjust the width of the back if using board other than 12 mm thickness
(All dimensions in millimetres)

Kestrel — *Falco tinnunculus*

Nestbox	Large open-fronted
Distribution/ status	Widespread, scarce only in northwest Scotland. Amber
Siting	At least 5 m from the ground with clear flight-path
Nest	Little or no material added, but hole may eventually become deep in prey remains and pellets
Eggs	4–5; white but often so heavily speckled reddish-brown that the white is obscured
Density	Unlikely to need more than 1 box per 100 hectares
Incubation	27–29 days, by female alone
Nestling	28–30 days
Broods	1

CBC/BBS population index

Kestrels need a clear view from, and a clear flight path to, the nest entrance. They will nest as low as 2.5 m but higher nests provide a better vantage point and more protection from human interference. Boxes facing the southeast quarter usually have higher occupancy rates, although shelter from extremes of the elements can be more important than aspect. As already mentioned, the box should be sited sloping backwards slightly, the eggs will remain secure in the darkest end of the box.

Fix a perch along the front of the box which extends well to one side and sweeps upwards. This will allow both adults and young to sit alongside the box with a good view in all directions.

Kestrels are now regularly seen in many urban areas and nest sites have been provided either by attaching standard boxes to the sides of buildings or other man-made structures. Some pairs may even nest on window ledges. Deeply recessed window ledges can be made more attractive to Kestrels by providing a front along the top of the window sill which will shelter the nest and keep the eggs from rolling out.

A Kestrel box designed by the Hawk & Owl Trust, fixed in a tree.

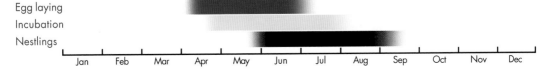

Egg laying											
Incubation											
Nestlings											
Jan	Feb	Mar	Apr	May	Jun	Jul	Aug	Sep	Oct	Nov	Dec

Papier-mâché nestboxes

House Martin

Swallow

Exploded view

Roof with inspection hole

Backing plate

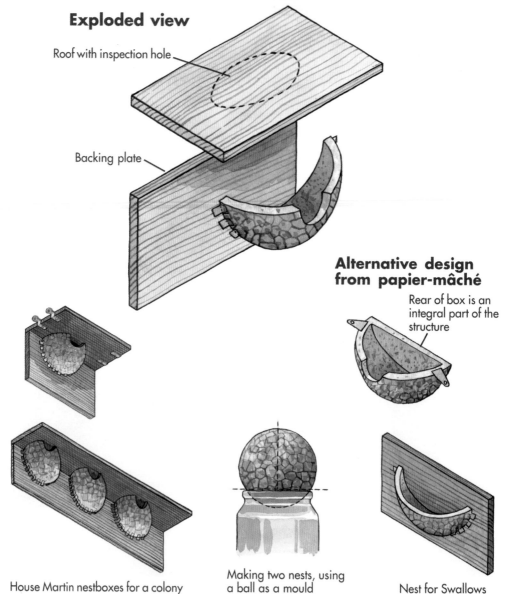

Alternative design from papier-mâché

Rear of box is an integral part of the structure

House Martin nestboxes for a colony

Making two nests, using a ball as a mould

Nest for Swallows

Papier-mâché nestboxes

Papier-mâché is an ideal material with which to construct artificial nest cups for House Martins and Swallows. It is easy to manipulate and surprisingly durable when coated on the outside with waterproof varnish. It is also very suitable for children to work with.

The exact shape of the nest cup is not critical, although typically it should form a quarter of a sphere of diameter 120 mm. To make a standard nest cup from papier-mâché:

1 Make a papier-mâché pulp by tearing up egg cartons or newspapers and soaking them overnight in water containing fabric conditioner.
2 Make a cup-shaped clay or Plasticine outer mould into which the papier-mâché can be pressed.
3 Grease the mould with Vaseline, squeeze out the excess water from the pulp and press it into place. Metal tabs for attaching the nest to the backing board can be incorporated into the cup at this stage.
4 Once dry, remove the cup from the mould.

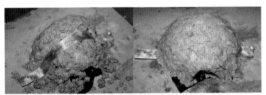

A bent metal strip embedded within the papier-mâché structure gives strength and provides fixing tabs. The second picture shows the completed box.

Alternatively, it is possible to make nest cups using an internal mould around which scraps of paper are glued together:

1 Make an inner mould using Plasticine or clay placed inside an old nest, or use a plastic ball of approximately 120 mm in diameter.
2 Cover the mould in Vaseline. If using a ball, it is best to rest it on the top of a jar.
3 Place strips of glued paper over the mould until the covering is at least 1 mm thick – water-based glue that becomes waterproof when dry is easy to use and gives good results.
4 Allow the glue to dry, then remove the mould. If you have used a ball as a mould, cut the dried nest into two halves to make two boxes.

If the nest is designed for use by House Martins, cut a semicircular nest entrance approximately 60 mm in diameter at the top edge of the cup. Do not worry about the precise dimensions, as the birds will add mud to the entrance to reduce it to the correct size.

For House Martins, attach the nest cups to wooden backing plates using more glued paper strips both inside and outside the nest. Attach a roof, again securing it using glue or paper strips. Once the glue is dry, cover the nest with waterproof varnish. The whole device can then be mounted under the eaves of a house by drilling holes in the back plate and using wing nuts, brackets or similar arrangements. This will allow safe and easy removal of the whole nest for inspection, recording and cleaning. If metal tabs are incorporated within the structure, the nest can be screwed directly under the eaves.

For Swallows, the nest cup is best attached to a single wooden backing plate, leaving the top completely open. The plate can then be fixed to a wall or a beam in a suitable location, such as the inside of a shed, barn or stable.

In places where there are no nearby muddy puddles or ponds, Swallows and House Martins can be assisted by the provision of artificial puddles. An upturned dustbin lid will be large enough. Fill it with a mixture including water, soil, lime, clay and (if possible) cow dung. Ensure the mixture remains moist and workable by adding more water in dry periods during the building season.

House Martin — *Delichon urbica*

Nestbox	Hole-entrance, special design
Distribution/ status	Present throughout the British Isles, though local in extreme northwest coastal areas. Amber
Siting	Under eaves, height at least 2 m
Nest	Lined with feathers and vegetable matter
Eggs	4–5; white
Density	Colonial nester. Increase numbers of nests as required
Incubation	14–16 days, by both sexes
Nestling	16–22 days
Broods	2 (3)

CBC/BBS population index

While House Martins naturally nest under ledges on cliffs, the eaves of houses provide good artificial substitutes. House Martins may be helped to nest both by providing a suitable site where they can build a natural nest and by providing the nest itself.

Suitable eaves need to have at least 15 cm of overhang to provide shelter. Because the nest of mud needs to adhere to the wall, a rough wall is better than a smooth one. A smooth wall may be roughened or a row of masonry nails may be placed about 12 cm below the eaves to aid nest attachment.

There is some suggestion, although not thoroughly investigated, that House Martins prefer light coloured eaves to darker ones.

House Martins look for landmarks and choose to nest in places that are easily identifiable and therefore often nest above windows or doors where their droppings can cause annoyance. By putting up a single box, you may attract other martins to nest nearby, with the box itself acting as a landmark. Thus, providing an artificial nest may help solve the problem of nests in the 'wrong' places.

Mount the box under the eaves of a house. If the house lacks eaves, a ledge about 120 mm wide can be fitted to the wall and boxes secured underneath. Ensure that eaves and ledges do not allow water to trickle into the nests. If possible, site boxes in a group rather than singly. Boxes may attract a new colony of House Martins, even if they are not themselves used.

A successful nest detached for inspection and to ring the young. Note the mud added to the entrance by the adult birds.

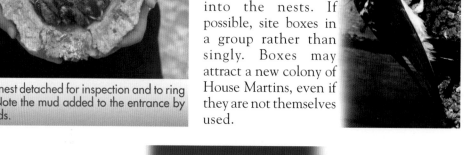

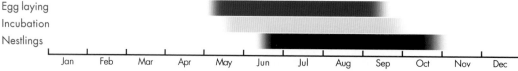

Egg laying											
Incubation											
Nestlings											
Jan	Feb	Mar	Apr	May	Jun	Jul	Aug	Sep	Oct	Nov	Dec

Swallow — *Hirundo rustica*

Nestbox	Open cup
Distribution/ status	Absent or scarce only in northwest Scotland. Prefers lowland farmland. Amber
Siting	On ledges or under rafters inside buildings
Nest	Lined with feathers
Eggs	4–6; white
Density	Colonial nester. As many nests as can be conveniently located
Incubation	14–16 days, mainly by female
Nestling	17–24 days
Broods	1–3

CBC/BBS population index

Swallows build their nests on ledges inside buildings. The 'ledge' which supports the nest may sometimes be as little as a nail projecting from a wall. The nest tends to be as high as possible within the building.

If no nesting site is available, a ledge, up to about 150 mm wide, can be fixed to a wall or roof timber high in a roof space. It does not matter if this roof space is in a low shed or a very tall barn. It will help if some beading is placed around the edges of the platform to help keep the nest in place.

Alternatively, artificial nests can be made in a similar way to those for House Martins using a mould that is between 100 mm and 130 mm in diameter. There is no need to make an entrance hole as the nest cup should be mounted with about 100 mm of headroom.

Artificial sites in buildings must have continuous access for the Swallows. This is not problem in open barns and sheds but in closed buildings, ensure that some entrance, such as a small, high window, is always open. Alternatively make a brick-sized hole in a wall.

As for House Martins, provide muddy puddles in dry weather.

A commercially produced, artificial nest mounted in the apex of an outbuilding roof.

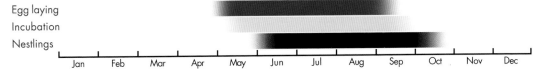

Egg laying
Incubation
Nestlings

Jan   Feb   Mar   Apr   May   Jun   Jul   Aug   Sep   Oct   Nov   Dec

Appendices

Species which may nest in nestboxes

The purpose of this guide is to give information about species which commonly use nestboxes of fairly standard designs. There are many other species which will use artificial sites. However, some of these sites require specialist equipment and need considerable investment of materials and manpower. Some species may only rarely use nestboxes. Other species may only nest in very restricted habitats. For completeness here, we list all species which are known to use artificial nest sites. It is intended that more information about box designs for these species will be added to the BTO website shortly (*www.bto.org*) . In the list below, species which are described in this book are printed in bold type.

Schedule 1 species are indicated †. The nests of Schedule 1 species must not be inspected or approached without a licence.

English Name	Scientific Name	Type of box
Barn Owl †	*Tyto alba*	Large hole entrance
Bearded Tit †	*Panurus biarmicus*	Wigwam (special design)
Black Guillemot (Tystie)	*Cepphus grylle*	Tunnel
Black-necked Grebe †	*Podiceps nigricollis*	Raft/island
Black Redstart †	*Phoenicurus ochruros*	Small open fronted
Black-throated Diver †	*Gavia arctica*	Raft/island
Blackbird	*Turdus merula*	Platform
Blue Tit	*Parus caeruleus*	Small hole entrance
Canada Goose	*Branta canadensis*	Raft/island
Coal Tit	*Parus ater*	Small hole entrance
Common Tern	*Sterna hirundo*	Raft/island
Coot	*Fulica atra*	Raft/island
Crested Tit †	*Parus cristatus*	Small hole entrance
Dipper	*Cinclus cinclus*	Small open fronted
Feral Pigeon	*Columba livia*	Large hole entrance
Goldeneye †	*Bucephala clangula*	Large hole entrance
Goosander	*Mergus merganser*	Large hole entrance
Goshawk †	*Accipiter gentilis*	Basket
Great Crested Grebe	*Podiceps cristatus*	Raft/island
Great Northern Diver †	*Gavia immer*	Raft/island
Great Spotted Woodpecker	*Dendrocopos major*	Medium hole entrance
Great Tit	*Parus major*	Small hole entrance
Green Woodpecker	*Picus viridis*	Medium hole entrance
Grey Wagtail	*Motacilla cinerea*	Small hole entrance
Greylag Goose †	*Anser anser*	Raft/island
Hobby †	*Falco subbuteo*	Basket
Hoopoe †	*Upupa epops*	Medium hole entrance
House Martin	*Delichon urbica*	Special
House Sparrow	*Passer domesticus*	Small hole entrance
Jackdaw	*Corvus monedula*	Large hole entrance
Kestrel	*Falco tinnunculus*	Large open front

Kingfisher †	*Alcedo atthis*	Tunnel
Kittiwake	*Rissa tridactyla*	Platform
Lesser Spotted Woodpecker	*Dendrocopos minor*	Medium hole entrance
Little Owl	*Athene noctua*	Large hole entrance
Little Tern †	*Sterna albifrons*	Platform
Long-eared Owl	*Asio otus*	Basket
Mallard	*Anas platyrhynchos*	Large hole entrance
Mandarin	*Aix galericulata*	Large hole entrance
Manx Shearwater	*Puffinus puffinus*	Tunnel
Marsh Tit	***Parus palustris***	Small hole entrance
Merlin †	*Falco columbarius*	Basket
Moorhen	*Gallinula chloropus*	Raft/island
Mute Swan	*Cygnus olor*	Raft/island
Nightjar	*Caprimulgus europaeus*	Scrape
Nuthatch	***Sitta europaea***	Small hole entrance
Osprey †	*Pandion haliaetus*	Basket
Oystercatcher	*Haematopus ostralegus*	Platform
Peregrine †	*Falco peregrinus*	Platform
Pied Flycatcher	***Ficedula hypoleuca***	Small hole entrance
Pied Wagtail	***Motacilla alba***	Small open front
Puffin	*Fratercula arctica*	Tunnel
Red-breasted Merganser	*Mergus serrator*	Tunnel
Red Kite †	*Milvus milvus*	Basket
Red-throated Diver †	*Gavia stellata*	Raft/island
Redstart	***Phoenicurus phoenicurus***	Small hole entrance
Ring-necked Parakeet	*Psittacula krameri*	Large hole entrance
Robin	***Erithacus rubecula***	Small open front
Roseate Tern †	*Sterna dougallii*	Tunnel
Sand Martin	*Riparia riparia*	Tunnel
Short-toed Treecreeper	*Certhia brachydactyla*	Special small hole entrance
Shelduck	*Tadorna tadorna*	Tunnel
Slavonian Grebe †	*Podiceps auritus*	Raft/island
Spotted Flycatcher	***Muscicapa striata***	Small open front
Starling	***Sturnus vulgaris***	Medium hole entrance
Stock Dove	***Columba oenas***	Large hole entrance
Storm Petrel	*Hydrobates pelagicus*	Tunnel
Swallow	***Hirundo rustica***	Open cup
Swift	***Apus apus***	Special hole entrance
Tawny Owl	***Strix aluco***	Large hole entrance
Tree Sparrow	***Passer montanus***	Small hole entrance
Treecreeper	*Certhia familiaris*	Special small hole entrance
Wheatear	*Oenanthe oenanthe*	Tunnel
Willow Tit	*Parus montanus*	Small hole entrance
Wood Duck	*Aix sponsa*	Large hole entrance
Wren	***Troglodytes troglodytes***	Small open front
Wryneck †	*Jynx torquilla*	Medium hole entrance

Addresses and Abbreviations

Organisations

BTO   British Trust for Ornithology, The Nunnery, Thetford Norfolk, IP24 2PU. (*www.bto.org*)

H&OT   The Hawk and Owl Trust, c/o Zoological Society of London, Regent's Park, London, NW1 4RY (*www.hawkandowl.org*)

JNCC   Joint Nature Conservation Committee, Monkstone House, City Road, Peterborough, PE1 1JY (*www.jncc.gov.uk*)

RSPB   Royal Society for the Protection of Birds, The Lodge, Sandy, Bedfordshire, SG19 2DL (*www.rspb.org.uk*)

    The Mammal Society, 2B Inworth Street, London SW11 3EP (*www.abdn.ac.uk/mammal*)

Other abbreviations

BBS   BTO/JNCC/RSPB Breeding Bird Survey

CBC   Common Birds Census

GBFS   Garden Bird Feeding Survey

IPMR   Integrated Population Monitoring Reporter

NRS   Nest Record Scheme

Further Reading

Animals Tracks, Trails and Signs. Brown, Lawrence & Pope. 1993. (Hamlyn)
A mine of information to help identify signs of animal activity including owl pellet contents and predation at nestboxes.

Bird Nests, Eggs and Nestlings of British and European Birds: with Northern Africa and the Middle East. Harrison & Castell. 2002. (HarperCollins)
Essential for identification of nests and eggs and other background information.

Boxes Baskets and Platforms. Dewar & Shawyer. 1996. (The Hawk & Owl Trust)
A comprehensive guide to artificial nest sites for owls and birds of prey in Britain.

The BTO/CJ Garden BirdWatch Book. Toms. 2003. (The British Trust for Ornithology)
A guide to bird species found in gardens together with advice about bird-friendly gardening. Draws heavily on records submitted by BTO/CJ Garden BirdWatchers.

The Garden Bird Book. Glue. 1982. (Macmillan)
Long out-of-print but still one of the best books about making your garden as valuable as it can be for bird life.

The New Atlas of Breeding Birds in Britain and Ireland: 1988–1991. Gibbons, Reid & Chapman. 1993 (T & AD Poyser, London)
The breeding distribution, numbers and habitats used by Britain and Ireland's birds.

The Population Status of Birds in the United Kingdom, Channel Islands and the Isle of Man: an analysis of conservation concern 2002–2007. Gibbons *et al.* 2002. British Birds 95:410–450
Latest review explaining the red, amber and green bird lists.

Photo-credits

The photographs are listed for each photographer. The number refers to the page and the letter to the specific photograph, from top left to bottom left, then top right to bottom right.

Derek Belsey:
7, 8a, 10a, 35c, 47a, 63d, 64c;
BTO collection:
58a.
Ian Carter:
53a;
Chris du Feu:
11b, 15b, 16a, 18b, 23a, 24b, 25a-c, 29a, 35a, 37c, 39a-c, 45b, 48b, 51b-c, 64a, 71a-b, 72a;
Darren Frost:
40b;
John Harding:
49a;
George Higginbotham:
37b, 42b, 44a, 45a, 59a, 63b, 65a, 66a, 70a, 72b, 72c;
Tommy Holden:
18c, 27, 33a, 38a-b, 40c, 41a-b, 42a, 42c, 47b, 48c-d, 51a, 52a-b, 60b, 63a, 64b, 67a, 69b-c, 73b;
Tony Jenkins:
40a;
Howard Lacey:
Front cover, 36a;
Chris Mead:
57b;
Rick & Vanessa Newman:
66b;

Dorothy Norman:
73a, 73c;
Jill Pakenham:
35b, 53b;
Colin Paton:
12, 13a, 17c, 18a, 19a-c, 20a, 21a-d, 22a-c, 23b, 24a, 32, 48a;
Graham Roberts:
Title page, 13b, 55a-b, 56b, 57a, 57c, 63c;
Colin Shawyer:
49b, 54b, 54d, 67b, 69a;
Moss Taylor:
56a;
Mike Toms:
54a, 54c, 59b;
Derek Toomer:
8c, 9a, 11a, 17b;
Unknown contributor (to an earlier edition)
23a;
David Waistell:
8b, 36b, 61a;
Nicholas Watts:
60a;
Mike Weston:
37a, 43a;
Ken Woodgate:
17a;

~~~~~~~~~~~~~~~~~~~~~